Twayne's English Authors Series

EDITOR OF THIS VOLUME

Arthur F. Kinney

University of Massachusetts

Richard Brome

TEAS 290

Reader, lo heere thou wilt two faces finde,
One of the body, t'other of the Minde ;
This by the Graver so, that with much strife
Wee thinke Brome dead, hee's drawne so to the life
That by's owne pen's done so ingeinously
That who reads it, must thinke hee nere shall dy .
                                                A·B·
        T. Crosse sculpsit.

Richard Brome

RICHARD BROME

By CATHERINE M. SHAW

University of Saskatchewan

TWAYNE PUBLISHERS
A DIVISION OF G. K. HALL & CO., BOSTON

Copyright © 1980 by G. K. Hall & Co.

Published in 1980 by Twayne Publishers,
A Division of G. K. Hall & Co.
All Rights Reserved

Printed on permanent/durable acid-free paper and bound
in the United States of America

First Printing

Frontispiece reproduced from original in
The Henry E. Huntington Library and Art Gallery

Library of Congress Cataloging in Publication Data

Shaw, Catherine M
Richard Brome.

(Twayne's English authors series ; TEAS 290)
Bibliography: p. 163–166.
Includes index.
1. Brome, Richard, d. 1652? —
Criticism and interpretation.
YR2439.B5Z87   822'.4   79–24523
ISBN 0–8057–6783–5

To the Memory of My Mother
Elizabeth Shaw

Contents

About the Author

Catherine M. Shaw is at present an Associate Professor with the English Department, University of Saskatchewan, Saskatoon. She has previously taught at the Universities of Illinois and California and has been a Visiting Professor at the University of British Columbia, Concordia, and McGill. The author of numerous articles on Shakespeare and his contemporaries, Professor Shaw has also written *'Some Vanity of Mine Art': The Masque in English Renaissance Drama*, University of Salzburg, 1980, and has edited *The Old Law* by Middleton and Rowley to be part of the Nottingham Drama Texts.

Statement

Variously interpreted as a typical Elizabethan comic playwright, a Caroline wit, or a bawdy precursor of Restoration drama, Richard Brome is the most seriously underrated comic dramatist of the seventeenth century. Professor Catherine M. Shaw helps to correct this situation in her detailed reexamination of his life and works. After analyzing those primary documents from which his biography must be reconstructed, she discusses Brome's apprenticeship to Ben Jonson and his later, mature work, finding in his bawdy jests, ingeniously complicated plots, and open satires a comic artist who turns to parody nearly every form and character he touches. In her discovery of his inversion of comic genres, Professor Shaw provides an especially useful way to reassess an English Renaissance writer whose works have suffered undeserved neglect.

ARTHUR F. KINNEY

Preface

Of the many significant Tudor and Stuart dramatists, Richard Brome has been the most neglected. We may hope that one day some perceptive stage producer may recognize his worth and mount a modern production of any of Brome's plays which so delighted his own and successive ages. Meantime, in *Richard Brome* my aim has been to provide the scholar and the critical reader with a close analysis of each play both as literature and as theatrical composition so as to give a balanced and comprehensive view of his comic art.

Although not strictly chronologically, Richard Brome developed from a writer of romantic comedy spiced with incidental caricature and parody into a first-rate farceur and satirist. In addition, he became a remarkably innovative dramatist. Thus, the division of the plays into chapters in this study is on a generic or subgeneric basis, according to which dramatic impression is dominant—seriocomic, comic-satirical, satiric-farcical—and, within each, attention is paid to features of his art which show originality. Chapter 8 then provides a survey of important critical opinions of Brome's position as a seventeenth-century playwright, an assessment of his place in the history of English drama and of his technical strengths and weaknesses, and a revaluation of his artistic worth.

Unfortunately, there are only two of Brome's plays, *The Antipodes* and *The Jovial Crew*, available in modern critical editions although others are waiting in the wings. An inadequate three-volume old-spelling edition was printed in London in 1873 but it provides neither introduction nor notes, and, as the editor paginated the plays in the first two volumes according to first-edition divisions and the third consecutively, it offers no clear form for citation. In this study, for consistency first editions of all Brome's works have been used and for facility references to the plays are given by act and scene as well as by signature. Although spelling has been modernized, original capitalization and punctuation has been adhered to as closely as possible.

For their kindness in allowing me to use their resources, I wish to thank the directors and their staffs of the British Library and the Huntington Library. I am especially grateful to the late Professor T. J. B. Spencer for allowing me to use as yet unpublished material at the Shakespeare Institute at the University of Birmingham, England. To Professor Helene Koon I am also grateful for her editorial assistance and critical judgment.

CATHERINE M. SHAW

University of Saskatchewan

Chronology

1590 (?) Birth of Richard Brome.

1614 Jonson's *Bartholomew Fair;* reference to Brome in Induction.

1623 (?) Possible early date for *Christianetta* (lost; collaboration with Chapman?).

1623 *A Fault in Friendship*, written by "Young Johnson and Broome," licensed (lost).

1626 (?) Possible early date for *The New Academy*.

1628 Name appears in June 30 list of Queen of Bohemia's Players.

1629 (?) Conjectured date for first version of *The City Wit*.

1629 Brome's *The Love-sick Maid* (lost) acted "with extraordinary applause" by the King's Men at Blackfriars. Jonson's first version of "Ode on Himself" in which he complains about audience preference for "Brome's sweepings." *The Northern Lass* acted by the King's Men.

1631 Brome answers petition of complaint filed by John Bonus.

1631– Conjectured date for *The Queen's Exchange*.
1632

1632 *The Northern Lass* published with commendatory poem by Jonson. *The Novella* written for the King's Men.

1632– *The Weeding of Covent-Garden* written for the King's
1633 Men.

1634 *The Late Lancashire Witches*, a collaboration with Thomas Heywood, written for the King's Men and published. Conjectured date for other collaboration with Heywood, *The Life and Death of Sir Martin Skink* (lost) and for *The Apprentice's Prize* (lost; also a collaboration with Heywood?). Possible later date for *Christianetta* (lost). Brome approached to write for the King's Revels at Salisbury Court.

1634–1635	*The Sparagus Garden* produced at Salisbury Court.
1635	July 20, Brome signs contract to write exclusively for Salisbury Court then occupied by the King's Revels. Conjectured date for *The New Academy*.
1635–1636	*The Queen and Concubine* written for King's Revels.
1636–1637	Plague closes London theaters from May 1636 until October 1637.
1637	*The English Moor* written for Salisbury Court. Writes verses for Thomas Nabbes's *Microcosmus*, Thomas Jordan's *Poetical Varieties*, and Shakerley Marmion's *Cupid and Psyche*.
1637–1639	*The City Wit* revised.
1638	Contract with Salisbury Court ends in July; new one offered in August. *The Damoiselle* written for King's Revels. Conjectured date for *The Love-sick Court*. *The Antipodes* written for Beeston's Boys at the Phoenix but produced at Salisbury Court.
1638–1639	Conjectured date for *Wit in a Madness* (lost).
1639	Brome joins Phoenix company. *A Mad Couple Well Match't* written for Beeston's Boys. Edits John Fletcher's *Monsieur Thomas* for Phoenix company.
1640	February 12, Salisbury Court company files complaint against Brome for breach of contract. March 6, Brome answers suit. March 19, Stationers' Register licenses *The Sparagus Garden, The Antipodes,* and *Wit in a Madness* (lost). *The Court Begger* written for Beeston's Boys. Verses written for John Tatham's *The Fancies Theatre* and Humphrey Mill's *A Night Search*.
1641	*A Jovial Crew* written for Beeston's Boys.
1642	September 2, theaters closed by Parliament. *The Sparagus Garden* and *The Antipodes* published.
1647	Contributes poem eulogizing John Fletcher to First Folio of Beaumont and Fletcher.
1649	Writes elegy for and possibly edits *Lachrymae Musarum*. Conjectured date for commendatory poem to William Cavendish for his play *The Variety* (pub. 1649).

1652   *A Jovial Crew* published.
1652–   Death of Richard Brome.
1653
1653   *Five New Plays (A Mad Couple Well Match't, The Novella, The Court Begger, The City Wit, The Damoiselle)* printed for Alexander Brome.
1657   *The Queen's Exchange* printed for Henry Brome. *Five New Plays (The English Moor, The Love-sick Court, The Weeding of Covent-Garden, The New Academy, The Queen and Concubine)* printed for Henry Brome.

CHAPTER 1

The Man and His Plays

R ICHARD Brome was one of the merriest of the many playwrights whose names immortalize the theater of Renaissance England. He was also a prolific writer. During his dramatic career (c. 1623-42) he may have presented as many as nineteen comedies to various acting companies and possibly collaborated in another six, although of these only sixteen are extant. Robust, popular with his contemporary audience (if somewhat bawdy for the Victorian critics), most of Brome's plays filled the Caroline stage with realistic glimpses into middle-class and often vulgar lower-class London life. And even when set outside familiar surroundings, their performances still held the mirror up to human idiosyncrasy and folly, while at the same time they depicted man's frailties with a healthy grin and his romantic nature with understanding and delight. Only his pet peeves, the court dramatists and their coterie whom he considered unprofessional and self-serving, were attacked with blunt and caustic wit.

The precise dates of composition have not been established for his plays, but the publication record gives some indication of chronology. Even this, however, is not conclusive, for only five were printed in his lifetime: *The Northern Lass* (1632), *The Late Lancashire Witches* (1634, in collaboration with Thomas Heywood), *The Sparagus Garden* (1642), and *The Antipodes* (1642), and, curiously enough, *A Jovial Crew* (1652), ten years after Parliament closed the theaters.

The other eleven extant plays were not published until after Brome's death in late 1652 or early 1653.[1] *Five New Plays*, edited posthumously by Alexander Brome (no relation) in 1653, includes *A Mad Couple Well Match't, The Novella, The Court Begger, The City Wit,* and *The Damoiselle.* In 1657, Henry Brome (also no relation) published a quarto edition of *The Queen's Exchange* and then, because this volume sold so well, brought out the second *Five New Plays* in 1659. This volume includes *The English Moor, The Love-sick Court, The Covent-Garden Weeded, The New Academy,* and *The Queen and Concubine.*

I   A Reconstructed Biography

Almost nothing is known of Brome's personal life. No records of birth or death have been uncovered, but recent scholarly detective work has revealed a few details, and some conjectures can be drawn from various plays. He seems to have been connected with Ben Jonson by 1614 from the lines spoken by the Stage-Keeper in the Induction to *Bartholomew Fair:*

But for the whole *Play,* will you have the truth on it? (I am looking, lest the *Poet* hear me, or his man, Master *Broome,* behind the Arras) it is like to be a very conceited scurvy one, in plain English.[2]

The word "man" might suggest that he was in his early twenties at the time and was thus born about 1590, but as Gerald Eades Bentley points out, "Such methods of dating are only acts of desperation. There is no definite fact in Brome's career to make a birth-date of 1575 or 1595 impossible."[3]

His place of birth also remains a mystery, but the skill with which he handles country dialects might suggest that, although he certainly knew the city well, he was not originally a Londoner. It is possible (as has often been speculated about Shakespeare) that he joined a group of itinerant actors touring the provinces and arrived in London already modestly associated with the theatrical profession. That Brome was an actor has been argued convincingly by Professor Alwin Thayer.[4] His main authority is an item appearing in a royal warrant dated June 30, 1628, giving evidence of Brome's association with the Queen of Bohemia's company, better known as Lady Elizabeth's Men.[5] This troupe was on tour frequently between 1610 and 1614, a fact which gives weight to the speculation that Brome joined the company when it was in the provinces and, after coming under Jonson's watchful eye, settled into the playhouse milieu. In this case, he was one of the actors when he stood "behind the Arras" in *Bartholomew Fair,* rather than a menial as the word "man" might suggest. Furthermore, although Jonson's closest associations were with the King's Men, he gave this particular play to

Lady Elizabeth's Men for performance by Nathan Field, one of his early actor-playwright protégés. Field's name, as well as Brome's, occurs in Jonson's text.[6]

Perhaps, then, Brome came to London as an actor sometime before 1614 and, while in some service to Jonson, impressed the playwright as a bright young man and was encouraged and helped by the older dramatist until he could advance from actor to playwright as Jonson himself had done in the late 1590s. A 1623 office-book of the Master of the Revels gives some support to this in a notice of the license for *A Fault in Friendship* written by "Young Johnson and Brome,"[7] and Bentley indicates that *The New Academy* may have been written as a "rival attraction" to James Shirley's *The School of Compliment*, licensed in 1625, because of the similarities. In that case, it also belongs to Brome's period of apprenticeship to Jonson.[8] Another play with a close resemblance to Jonson's style is *The City Wit*, probably written about 1628-29 although revised in 1637-39.[9] Like *The Alchemist*, it is a "cony-catching" drama consisting of a series of disguises undertaken for the purpose of cozening a succession of gulls. Brome's relationship with his mentor apparently ended about this time.

While little is known of Brome's life outside of the theater, Bentley cites three records which, although the name is a common one, possibly indicate Brome was married three times and had at least one child:

1616, July 8—'Richard Brome & Frances Lott widow' mar. St. Michael Bassishaw. (Challen, *Marriages*)
1627, Dec. 4—'Richard Brome & Joan Dylke, L. vg.' mar. St. Gregory by St. Paul. (Challen)
1642, Sept 16—'Lucia Daughter of Richard Brome esq[r] and Sara uxor' chris, St. G.F.[10]

There is other evidence that he was married and had a family. In Brome's answer to a Bill of Complaint brought against him by the Salisbury Court Theatre in 1640, the poet makes reference to the hardships suffered by him and his family because the Salisbury Court company had refused to pay him for his services when the theaters were closed during the plague of 1636-37.[11]

Penury seems to have plagued him most of his life. In late 1638 or early 1639 he complained that the company slighted two plays he had written for them, although he repeatedly asked them for aid because he was very sick. The closing of the theaters in 1642, of course, ended his theatrical livelihood. He makes specific reference to his poverty in the dedicatory letter to Lord Thomas Stanley which precedes the quarto publication of *A Jovial Crew* in 1652. He says he needs not only a judge for his work but also a patron.

> . . . *We all know* [he goes on], Beggars *use to flock to great mens Gates. And, though my fortune has cast me in that Mold, I am poor and proud; and preserve the humour of him, who could beg for anything, but* great Boons, *such as are your kind* Acceptance *and* Protection.
>
> (A 2^r)

After the closing of the theaters, Brome appears to have written very little: he contributed a poem eulogizing John Fletcher for the first folio of Beaumont and Fletcher's *Works* in 1647 and two years later wrote an elegy for, (and probably edited) *Lachrymae Musarum*, a collection of poems lamenting the death of Henry Hastings, son to the Earl of Huntingdon. Another commendatory poem, "To My Lord of Newcastle, on his play called *The Variety*" (a drama printed with *The Country Captain* in 1649), was probably written in the same year but did not appear in print until the 1659 publication of Brome's own second group of plays. Just before Brome's death *A Jovial Crew* was printed with the dedicatory epistle to Lord Stanley mentioned above.

Of those whom Brome counted among his friends, Ben Jonson, Thomas Dekker, Thomas Heywood, John Ford, and Robert Chamberlain predeceased him. Others, like James Shirley and John Tatham, who like him were denied opportunities by the Commonwealth restrictions on theaters, also respected Brome and wrote verses commending the quality of his drama. Alexander Brome was more of a poet and editor than playwright, but his admiration of his namesake's work led him to publish the first group of five plays and to write verses prefacing the second. He concludes his dedication to *"the late facetious* Poet" with:

> *Poor* he came into the world, and *poor* went out.
> His *soul* and *body* higher powers claim,
> There's nothing left to play with, but his *name;*
> Which you may freely *toss;* he all endures.
> But as you use his name, so'll others yours.[12]

II *Brome and Jonson: Rival Dramatists*

When Richard Brome's first plays appeared on the English boards in 1629, they were instant successes, and Alexander Brome's words indicate something of the way in which those who resented his popularity chose to attack him—through his name and through his apparently lower station in society. The first of these attacks came, somewhat ironically, from the very man who had been Brome's mentor—Ben Jonson.

Early in 1629, Ben Jonson's *The New Inn* was presented by the King's Men at Blackfriars. The play was a dismal failure. Such rejection by the audience would be enough under the best of circumstances to incite a roar of outrage from the aging playwright. Insult, however, was quickly added to injury. Edmond Malone has recorded for us what happened just a few weeks later:

Very soon indeed after the ill success of Jonson's piece, the King's Company brought out at the same theatre a new play called *The Lovesick Maid, or The Honour of Young Ladies,* which was licensed by Sir Henry Herbert, on the 9th of February, 1628-9, and acted with extraordinary applause. This play, which was written by Jonson's own servant, Richard Brome, was so popular, that the managers of the King's Company, on the 10th of March, presented the Master of the Revels with the sum of two pounds, "on the good success of *The Honour of Ladies*"; the only instance I have met with of such a compliment being paid him.[13]

Jonson's response was instantaneous and scathing. In "Ben Jonson's Ode to Himself" he attacks the taste of the contemporary audience by saying they "love lees" and not "lusty Wine" in the theater. He goes on, "Broome's sweeping do as well. There as his Master's Meal."[14] Certainly if Brome's servant-disciple relationship with Jonson had not terminated before this time, Jonson's anger would be enough to push the young dramatist out on his own then for although Jonson's attack was principally against the critics of the play, Richard Brome bore the brunt of it. Jonson's loyal friends, his "sons," stood behind him. One, Thomas Randolph, addressed an ode to his master in which he begged Jonson to ignore an audience that could be content with what Brome "swept" from Jonson.[15] Just how long the estrange-

ment between Jonson and Brome lasted is difficult to tell.
Certainly it was over when *The New Inn* was published in 1631,
for Jonson appended his "Ode to Himself" to this issue with the
reference to Brome omitted. By 1632 they were obviously good
friends again because Jonson wrote the following lines as part of
a commendatory poem to *The Northern Lass* when it was
published that year. They are addressed "To my old Faithful
Servant: and (by his continued Virtue) my loving Friend":

> *I had you for a Servant, once,* Dick Brome;
> *And you performed a Servant's faithful parts:*
> *Now, you are got into a nearer room,*
> *Of Fellowship, professing my old Arts.*
> *And you do do them well, with good applause,*
> *Which you have justly gained from the* Stage
> *By observation of those Comic Laws*
> *Which I, your* Master, *first did teach the Age.*
> *You learned it well; and for it served your time*
> *Apprenticeship: which few do now-a-days.*
> *Now each Court-Hobby-horse will wince in rhyme;*
> *Both learned, and unlearned, all write* Plays.[16]

The fate of *The Love-sick Maid* and *The Northern Lass,*
however, suggests that the resentment against Brome felt either
by Jonson or more probably by his supporters had gone further
than mere verbal attack. First, we might ask why such an
approved play as *The Love-sick Maid* was never published. It is
true that the most powerful companies often withheld their most
popular plays from print but, in this case, only one further
performance of the play is recorded (April 6, 1629), and
although the title appears in a 1641 list of plays owned by the
King's Men and again in a list appearing in the Stationers'
Register in 1653,[17] the play is not extant. Second, from its initial
performance on July 29, 1629, *The Northern Lass* was also a
tremendously popular play. Yet, judging from Brome's dedication to Richard Holford which prefaces the 1632 edition, there
was a period within these three years during which the play was
withheld from the stage. The author says:

Rich Friends may send you rich Presents, while poor ones have nothing
but good wishes to present you. Though I be one of the last rank, and

therefore cannot do like the first, yet it is my ambition to bring more than bare wishes with me, to one, of whom I have received real favours. A Country Lass I present you, that *Minerva*-like was a brain-born Child; and *Jovially* begot, though now she seeks her fortune. She came out of the cold North, thinly clad: But *Wit* had pity on her; *Action* apparalled her, and Plaudits clapped her cheeks warm. She is honest, and modest, though she speak broad: And though *Art* never strung her tongue; yet once it yielded a delightful sound: which gained her many Lovers and Friends, by whose good liking she prosperously lived, until her late long Silence, and Discontinuance (to which she was compelled) gave her justly to fear their loss, and her own decay.

(A 2^{r-v})

Plague closed the theaters in the spring of 1631, but this can hardly be held accountable for the "long silence" to which Brome refers. As Bentley points out, none of the material in the play "could be called offensive,"[18] yet it was not licensed for printing until March 24, 1632.[19] Why then, had *The Northern Lass* been compelled to "Discontinuance"? A possible and not entirely speculative answer is that the injury to Jonson's ego inflicted by the success of *The Love-sick Maid* had been further aggravated by yet another success, *The Northern Lass*, only five months later. Jonson's association with the King's Men had been a long and mutually satisfactory one. Of his earlier plays, such successes as *Every Man in His Humour* and *Volpone* had been presented under their auspices and from *The Alchemist* on, every play except *Bartholomew Fair* (Lady Elizabeth's, 1614) and *The Tale of a Tub* (Queen Henrietta's, 1633) had been given to the men of the Globe and Blackfriars. In addition, and in spite of Jonson being in the twilight of his career, the name Ben Jonson was the most revered among literary men, particularly those who declared themselves members of the Tribe of Ben.[20] Perhaps, then, under these circumstances, it was not difficult for Jonson's supporters to persuade the officers of the King's Men to withdraw the Brome plays, whose success had given such injury to their mentor.

From 1632 until Jonson's death in 1637, Brome's relationship with Jonson showed no further sign of strain, but this early friction between Brome and his former master was considered serious enough and common enough knowledge for Alexander Brome to refer to it in his prefatory poem to Brome's last play *A*

Jovial Crew, written in 1641. Part of Alexander Brome's praise for the playwright reads:

> . . . *I love thee* for thy *Name*;
> *I love thee* for thy Merit, and thy *Fame*:
> *I love thee* for thy *neat* and *harmless wit*,
> Thy *Mirth* that does so *clean* and *closely hit*.
> Thy *luck* to *please* so well: who could go faster?
> At first to be the *Envy* of thy *Master*.[21]

Even when the conflict was not mentioned specifically by later writers, its occurrence gave rise to an unfortunately condescending attitude by some contemporary playwrights and a tendency to belittle Brome for his lowly beginnings. The address "To the Readers" which prefaces the 1659 edition of *Five New Plays* refers to this attitude and comes to Brome's defense:

And yet there are a sort (one would wonder there should be) who think they lessen this *Author's* worth when they speak the relation he had to *Ben. Jonson*. We very thankfully embrace the Objection, and desire they would name any other Master that could better teach a man to write a good Play.

Then, after quoting Jonson's verse letter to John Selden, the writer continues:

It seems (whate'er we think) *Ben* thought it a diminution for no man to attend upon his Muse. And were not already the Ancients too much trod on, we could name famous wits who served far meaner Masters than *Ben Johnson*.[22]

Richard Brome does not appear to have made any specific retaliatory statements in his own defense. Rather, he acknowledged his debt to Jonson. In the revised version of *The City Wit*, the playwright added a prologue in which he says:

> *The Schoolmaster that never yet besought ye,*
> *Is now become a suitor, that you'll sit,*
> *And exercise your Judgement with your wit,*
> *On this our Comedy, which in bold Phrase,*
> *The Author says has passed with good applause*

> *In former times. For it was written, when*
> *It bore just Judgement, and the seal of* Ben.
>
> (A 2ᵛ)

On occasion he also emphasized his indebtedness by deliberately making obvious references to the older playwright's works. A clear allusion to *The Alchemist,* for example, occurs in *The Sparagus Garden* when Money-Lack says to Brittle-ware, ". . .Yet thou and I *Jack* have been always confident of each other, and have wrought friendly and closely together, as ever *Subtle* and his Lungs did. . ." (D 1ᵛ; II,iii).

Although Richard Brome was not exactly an unknown in the theatrical world when *The Love-sick Maid* caused such controversy, the publicity attendant upon it certainly gave his career an unexpected boost, and there is every indication that, after *The Northern Lass,* Brome was well on his way to becoming one of the most popular dramatists of his age. In fact, it would be fair to say that with the exception of James Shirley and Philip Massinger, Brome was not only the most popular but the best of the Caroline playwrights. The high acclaim with which *The Northern Lass* was received by his contemporaries is indicated by some of the poems which prefaced its 1632 publication. In addition to Jonson's testimony that his former servant had learned the "Comic Laws" and that he deserved the "good applause" which his play was accorded, playwrights as well known as John Ford and Thomas Dekker praised both the work and the author.

III   *Brome and the Acting Companies*

During the early 1630s, Brome was closely associated with the King's Men; both *The Queen's Exchange* (1631–32?) and *The Novella* were written for them, and Bentley provides ample evidence that *The Weeding of Covent-Garden* (1632–33) belonged to King's as well.[23] In July 1634, according to the official records of the Lord Chamberlain's office, he was collaborating with Thomas Heywood on *The Late Lancashire Witches,* produced by the same company.[24]

At this point he appears to have joined the Red Bull players for a brief time. Professor Ann Haaker has published two documents which include references to Brome's service with that company.

The first is a Request Bill of Complaint filed on February 12, 1640, charging Brome with breach of contract; the other his answer, dated March 6, 1640,[25] stating that when Richard Gunnell, representing the Salisbury Court company, approached him to write for them in 1634, the playwright was attached to "the company of the Red Bull players being the Prince's highness servants." Since he signed the contract with the Salisbury Court theater, then occupied by the King's Revels, in July 1635, he could only have been with the Red Bull company less than a year. There is, of course, the possibility of some overlapping in his associations with the two companies, in which case he may have had a slightly longer attachment, but one would think that if his services were in demand by both theaters he would have mentioned it. Although no specific plays are ascribed to Brome's time with the Red Bull company, Bentley suggests the lost plays, *Life and Death of Sir Martin Skink* and *Christianetta,* may belong to this period.[26]

The success of *The Sparagus Garden,* produced at Salisbury Court in late 1634 or early 1635, further stimulated the company's interest in Brome and the association between playwright and theater was formalized in July 1635. This contract with the King's Revels at Salisbury Court, a theater at the bottom of what is now Dorset Street, obliged the dramatist to write exclusively for them. He was to compose three plays a year for three years, for which he would receive fifteen shillings a week plus one day's profit from each play.[27] It would appear that all went well between company and playwright for a little over a year, during which Brome presented two plays to the acting company, *The Queen and Concubine* and one other, probably *The New Academy.*[28] Unfortunately, on May 12, 1636, all the theaters in London were closed because of one of the most protracted outbreaks of plague. They remained dark until October 1637, and the closure ruined the King's Revels company. Bentley testifies that "there are no records of a London King's Revels after the plague of 1636-37, and I think we may take for granted that none existed."[29] When the Salisbury Court opened again it was occupied by Queen Henrietta's Men. Philip Bordinat, citing from the *Dramatic Records of Sir Henry Herbert,* says the new company was formed from the residue of the King's Revels plus "the chief members of [Christopher] Beeston's old company at the Cockpit, Queen

Henrietta's Men."[30] Brome wrote only one play, *The English Moor* (1637), between the reopening of the theater and the termination of the first agreement. In his response to the complaint brought against him for breach of contract, Brome admits that technically he did owe the company two plays, "in lieu of which," he states, "he hath made diverse scenes in old revived plays *for them*. . . ."[31] One of these was probably the revision of *The City Wit*.

Much of the wrangling and bad feelings between Richard Brome and the Salisbury Court people had its origins in the differing opinions as to what the obligations of each party were during the time the theater was closed and the subsequent conflicting statements as to what extent the theatrical company had fulfilled its obligations. Yet Salisbury Court must have recognized the worth of Brome, for, in spite of their differences, the producers obviously did not want to lose his services. When Brome's contract came to an end in July 1638 they offered him a renewal, but apparently the feelings between playwright and company remained uncongenial, because in 1639 their association was terminated. Under the second arrangement with Salisbury Court, however, Brome wrote *The Damoiselle* (1638), *The Antipodes* (1638), *The Love-sick Court* (1638), and possibly *Wit in a Madness*.[32] As the plays written under the earlier contract seem to be accounted for, *Wit in a Madness* may be one of those plays Brome said he wrote for the company between "Hillary Term [January 23–February 12] 1638" and Easter 1639, which the company chose to "slight."[33] Such treatment of his work, plus the scorn and reproach which he says were heaped upon his person, made him break off all relations with the Salisbury Court theater and turn to another group with which he could be happy and congenial—to the King and Queen's Young Players, owned by his friends the Beestons, then playing at the Phoenix (also known as the Cockpit) in Drury Lane.

As further evidence of his unhappiness with his treatment by Queen Henrietta's Men, Brome had already tried in 1638 to give one of his plays, *The Antipodes*, to the rival company at the Phoenix. This note was appended to the 1642 edition of the play:

Courteous Reader, *You shall find in this Book more than was presented on the* Stage, *and left out of the* Presentation *for the superfluous length (as some of the* Players *pretended) I thought good that all should be inserted according to the allowed* Original: *and as it was, at first, intended for the* Cockpit Stage, *in the right of my most deserving friend Mr.* William Beeston, *unto whom it properly appertained; and so I leave it to thy perusal, as it was generally applauded, and well acted at* Salisbury Court. *Farewell,* Ri. Brome.

(L 4ᵛ)

Aside from Jonson, probably no one was more professionally compatible with Brome than the Beestons. Christopher Beeston had acted with William Shakespeare and Richard Burbage as early as 1598, built the Phoenix Theatre in 1617, and had over forty years experience in the theater before his death in 1638. When his son William took over the King and Queen's Young Players, they continued to be called Beeston's Boys rather than by their more formal title. Less is known of William's early theatrical experience, but he was probably apprenticed to his father, and it was he who obtained Brome's services for the players in Drury Lane.

Brome had great admiration for both Beestons and paid them tribute in the epilogue to *The Court Begger.* Swaynwit, who speaks the epilogue, takes the opportunity to express the playwright's distaste for those writers, particularly "University Scholars," who rely upon others' wits to bolster up their plays with intruded songs and interludes. He goes on:

But this small Poet vents none but his own, and his by whose care and directions this Stage is governed, who has for many years both in his father's days and since, directed Poets to write & Players to speak, till he trained up these youths here to what they are now. Aye, some of them from before they were able to say a grace of two lines long to have more parts in their pates than would fill so many Dryfats.

(S 8ʳ⁻ᵛ)

Obviously the stage governor is William Beeston. Swaynwit continues, "And to be serious with you, if after all this, by the venomous practice of some, who study nothing more than his destruction, he should fail us, both Poets and Players would be at loss in reputation." For a short time Beeston, at the order of Sir Henry Herbert, was replaced as the head of the King and Queen's Young Players by William Davenant, a court dramatist so heartily disliked by the professional playwrights[34] that there can be no doubt that, through Swaynwit, Brome is attacking

Davenant's attempt to use court influence to forward his ambitions to govern his own professional theater.

Richard Brome's alliance with Beeston's Boys was the last of his playwrighting career, extending from some time after Easter 1639 until the theater was closed along with all the others in London on September 2, 1642. During this period he edited John Fletcher's *Monsieur Thomas* (1639) and presented three plays to the company: *A Mad Couple Well Match't* (1639), *The Court Begger* (1640), and *A Jovial Crew* (1641), one of his best and most popular comedies, although its pre-Commonwealth career was brief. From the comment in the dedication to Lord Stanley which prefaced the first edition, *A Jovial Crew* (1652) appears to have been the last play presented by the company before the final curtain dropped. In it, the playwright begs for aid, then says:

All the Arguments I can use to induce you to take notice of this thing of nothing, *is, that it had the luck to tumble last of all in the* Epidemical *ruin of the* Scene; *and now limps hither with a* wooden Leg, *to beg Alms at your hands.*

(A 2ᵛ)

And, indeed, 1642 was for Brome and for all professional playwrights *"the* Epidemical *ruin of the* Scene." Of his well-known contemporaries, ironically only William Davenant survived the interregnum period to write plays for the new Restoration audience.

IV *Friends and Associates*

Richard Brome's last years were spent in unhappy retirement. In the poem he contributed to *Lachrymae Musarum,* the collection elegizing the young Henry Hastings, Brome recalls happier times:

> Away, my *Muse,* or bid me hence from thee;
> No Subject for thy help, nor Work for me.
> This story yields. For, by thy dictates, I
> Never spilt Ink, except in Comedy;
> Which in the thronged Theatres did appear
> All mirth and laughter. . . .
> . . . .

> And (pardon me, *Thalia*) your sublime
> Spirit, since this vicissitude of Time
> Has found no cause to smile, nor have you been
> But Mourner-like, and but by Mourners seen.
> And, though you cannot express Sorrow, I
> Must be allowed to show Mortality;
> And grieve without your aid.[35]

Since there is no connection between Brome and the
Huntingdons, a wealthy royalist family, the provocation for the
collection must have come from others who contributed poems.
They may have asked him to edit the volume and contribute an
elegy out of respect for his reputation and concern for his
diminished state. Certainly there are interrelationships between
Brome and the other poets whose verses appear in the volume.
Robert Herrick and Sir Aston Cokayne both had friendly
connections with another of the elegists, Charles Cotton, to
whose father Brome had dedicated his edition of Fletcher's
Monsieur Thomas in 1639. Both had also, along with Brome,
written commendatory verses to the first folio of Beaumont and
Fletcher (1647), and Cokayne wrote a Praeludium for Brome's
Five New Plays in 1653. Alexander Brome, the editor of that
collection, was another contributor to *Lachrymae Musarum*.
John Hall and J. B., other elegists who honored the memory of
Henry Huntingdon, had also written verses for *A Jovial Crew*.
The direct link between these various poets and the Huntingdon
family, however, is probably Sir Aston Cokayne, who was close
enough to it to have accompanied Baron Loughborough, the
distinguished loyalist and uncle to the deceased youth, to the
Continent at the end of the first part of the civil war in 1646.

To these distinguished names associated with Richard Brome
we can add Thomas Dekker, James Shirley, and John Ford,
considered among the best of the Jacobean and Caroline
dramatists, as well as lesser playmakers such as Robert Chamberlain and John Tatham, all of whom at one time or another wrote
verses in praise of Brome and his comedies.[36] That his plays were
also popular with contemporary audiences is indicated by the
fact that most of their titles appear in lists protected for the
acting companies through the Lord Chamberlain. The continued
popularity into the Restoration of some of Brome's plays will be
discussed later, but it is interesting at this point to note into what

eminent company Brome's name was placed by the chronicler Edward Phillips in his comments on "Men of Note":

Poetry was never more Resplendent, nor never more Graced; wherein *Jonson, Silvester, Shakespeare, Beaumont, Fletcher, Shirley, Brome, Massinger, Cartwright, Randolph, Cleveland, Quarles, Carew, Davenant,* and *Suckling,* not only far excelled their own Countrymen, but the whole World besides.[37]

M. C. Bradbrook would see this association of Richard Brome with the likes of James Shirley as "a revolution from the day a half a century earlier when Robert Green, a Master of Arts, had considered it presumption for Shakespeare to take to the art of playwrighting!"[38] Perhaps, however, Shirley is the wrong person to single out for his acceptance of Brome as a fellow playwright despite Brome's lack of university training and court polish. An attitude of superiority was still shown by the court dramatists toward the professional playwrights, particularly by Davenant and Suckling, and, in turn, disdain toward the aristocratic playmakers shown by the professionals who had risen through the ranks of the theatrical world. Brome's pejorative view toward these writers is seen in the Prologue to *The Court Begger*:

> We've cause to fear yours, or the Poet's frown
> For of late days (he knows not how) you're grown,
> Deeply in love with a new strain of wit
> Which he condemns, at least disliketh it,
> And solemnly protests you are to blame
> If at his hands you do expect the same.

(N 4ᵛ)

Shirley, although a Cambridge graduate and attached to the household of Queen Henrietta Maria, was unlike those Brome condemns. He was a professional of the first order. Long associated with the Cockpit company, he shared Brome's disdain for the court wits:

> *Learning,* the File of *Poesie* may be
> Fetched from the *Arts* and *University*:
> But he that writes a *Play,* and good, must know,
> Beyond his Books, Men, and their Actions too.

And he commended his friend with

> Thy *Fancy's* Metal; and thy strain much higher
> Proof 'gainst their *Wit*, and what that dreads, the *Fire*.[39]

Strange bedfellows though they may seem, this professionalism banded Brome and Shirley together in their comic attacks against pretentiousness, hypocrisy, and affectation, albeit the brunt of these assaults was toward different levels of class-structured Caroline society. Douglas Sedge confirms that "in the main Brome's comedy reflects the life and manners of a Caroline bourgeois London, a counterpart of Shirley's upper-class society." With the possible exception of *The Queen and Concubine, The Queen's Exchange, The Love-sick Court*, and *A Jovial Crew*, all of Brome's plays have, to a greater or lesser extent, characteristics of citizen comedy. As for Shirley, "there is no serious place for the citizen in his plays. If he had an ideal it is that of an honestly cautious and industrious country gentleman who is characterized in ideal terms in *The Witty Fair One*."[40] Brome, on the other hand, knew most intimately the common man of the hustle and bustle of London and is at his best when peopling his stage with common men and using their language.

V   *Conclusion*

Such is the account of what is known and what can be speculated about the life of Richard Brome, his position in his profession, and his relations with his contemporaries and his age. The paucity of biographical record can be balanced by the wealth of information to be gleaned from his works and his professional attachments. As for his character, his own pronouncements and those made about him by his friends present a man of strong moral profile. Although he was unpretentious, the mask of humility which he appeared to adopt for himself was deceptive. Deprecatory self-consciousness was as often a pose for the satirist as Jonson's assumption of superiority was. Brome was proud of his craft and never ceased to delight in it. He was in every sense a professional. He could be as caustic and blunt as was Ben Jonson but, unlike his mentor, his fundamental attitude toward his fellow man was benevolent. Brome seems to have been able, with a few exceptions, to accept man as he was, with all his weaknesses and conceits. What he was unable to bear was any pretension to being other than mortal and flawed, but even in attack he was always witty and devoted to "sport[ing] with human follies, not with crimes."[41] Perhaps Alexander Brome said it best:

> I'll tell the World, I've read these poems o'er,
> And find them in so natural a vein
> Of clean, rich Fancy, in so pure a strain:
> That I may safely say, who does not love it,
> Can't for his life write anything above it.
> This witty Pen, this mirthful Comic style,
> Makes us at once both serious, and smile.
> Wraps serious truths in fab'lous mysteries,
> And thereby makes us merry, and yet wise.[42]

Only in the past twenty years or so has Richard Brome begun to receive the attention which the quality of his work deserves. Much of this is the result of Jonson's rise during this century to challenge Shakespeare as the most influential dramatist of the age. Interest in Jonson and Jonson's concern for artistic craft has led to consideration of his "sons" and their contribution to Renaissance drama. Although by no means a carbon copy of Jonson, Richard Brome is the most brilliant "son" not only because initially he followed his master but because he inherited Jonson's most precious talents—a willingness to experiment and innovate and an awareness of responsibility to his art. In the verses Brome wrote for the first folio of the plays of Beaumont and Fletcher (1647), he says:

> . . . Y'have your jeers: Sirs, no;
> But, in a humble manner, let you know
> Old serving-creatures oftentimes are fit
> T'inform young Masters.[43]

As R. W. Ingram has observed, for Brome "this was no idle brag; for he had as much to teach Caroline masters as he himself had had to learn from Jonson."[44] Although a worthy inheritor of both Jonson's comic legacy and the deeply embedded traditions of all English drama, Richard Brome also added much that was new to the Caroline stage and, after the interregnum, continued to influence the comic playwrights that followed him.

CHAPTER 2

The Ladies Take the Stage

I The Northern Lass

F EW dramatists receive the applause and critical acclaim for
an early work that Richard Brome did for *The Northern Lass,*
the play that caused so much flurry when it was acted in 1629.
The initial popularity of *The Lass* has already been attested to
and the continued performances both before and after the
Commonwealth period indicate its continued success.[1] In addition, from the time it first appeared in print until 1717, no fewer
than eight editions were published.

Jonson's commendatory poem to the first edition (1632) is
mainly concerned with welcoming his former servant into a
"nearer room of Fellowship" and attacking court would-be
playwrights who had not served their apprenticeship in the craft
of playmaking. John Ford, who signs himself "The *Authors* very
friend," directs his attention to the play and compares Brome's
work favorably with modish drama. *"The Court,"* he says,
"affords No newer fashion, or for Wit, or Words" than *"This
well-limb'd Poëm."*[2] Others, however, who contributed verses
indicate the reason for the play's instantaneous popularity—the
lass herself simply captivated the audience. Her *"naturall*
Beauties" and *"sweetnesse"* surpass, says St[ephen] Br[ome], all
others *"whose gaudy shewes take hold Of gazing eyes."*[3] Thomas
Dekker claims Brome's heroine as his "grandchild." *"Not
Lumpish-Cold,* [he declares] *as is her Clime. . . . Thy* Northern Lass *Our Southern proudest* Beauties *pass."*[4] Another,
identified only as F. T., says:

> *What! wilt thou prostitute thy* Mistress, *(Friend)*
> *And make so rich a Beauty common? What end*
> *Dost you propose? She was thine own, but now*

> *All will enjoy her free: 'tis strange that thou*
> *Canst brook so many rivals in thy Lass,*
> *Whose Wit and Beauty does her Sex surpass.*
> *I've learnt it; Thou hast tried her, found her chaste,*
> *And fear'st not that She'll lewdly be embraced:*
> *And now thou sendst her to be seen, and see*
> *If any be like fair, like good as She.*[5]

These comments leave no doubt that the focal point of *The Northern Lass* is its heroine. It is her story, her plight, into which all other romantic and satiric threads of the play are woven and, as we shall see, the lass stands at the head of a long line of Brome's skillfully drawn women.

Basically the lass's story is a simple one. Previous to the play's action, Sir Philip Luckless, while on a visit to the northern part of England, has jokingly suggested to her uncle that he would make a fine husband for Constance. Thinking him serious, the maiden has followed him to London only to find her erstwhile lover already betrothed to a wealthy widow, Mistress Fitchow. The narrative development of the play is concerned with sorting out this romantic triangle and the various other entanglements ancillary to it. The cross-plotting of fortunes and misfortunes is easily followed because each of the intrigues is structurally integrated into the main action centering on the heroine.

Trying to keep Sir Philip from a marriage to Fitchow, which he feels would be a mistake, Tridewell, another gentleman, goes to the widow hoping that by exaggerating Philip's unworthiness he can convince her to break off the betrothal. Upon seeing the lady, however, Tridewell falls in love with her himself and thus is given a much more important reason for preventing the wedding. If the Luckless-Fitchow-Tridewell triangle is resolved in Tridewell's favor, this would release Philip to be united with Constance. Tridewell is thus cast into the role of comic manipulator who, with the help of wily servants and coconspirators, manages to bring off the happy chain of events.

In keeping with a structure based upon multiple plotting which Brome uses frequently and well, *The Northern Lass* includes a third and bawdy element, or what Richard Levin calls "another level of tone or sensibility."[6] Although the introduction of the heroine and information concerning her being in London is delayed until the second act, the suspicion that some confusion exists in Philip's previous relationships with women is clearly established in Act I. A gentlewoman calls upon him rather suddenly and, when she has confirmed the rumor that Sir Philip is to be married, presents him with a plaintive little poem signed "Constance."

> *If pity, love, or thought of me,*
> *Live in your Breast I need not die.*
> *But if all those from thence be fled;*
> *Live you to know, that I am dead.*

$$(B\ 4^r;I,iv.)$$

His reaction is somewhat startling. Even while recognizing the verse as literate and the messenger as gentle, he assumes that the plea comes from a whore of his acquaintance. Pate, Philip's servant, learns that the woman has come in a coach accompanied by her own serving man but he is convinced the two are pimps. He plans to outwit them by arranging for their "Constance" to meet that evening with his "master" who will be, in fact, Anville, a lecherous braggart and governor to Widgine, Mistress Fitchow's witless young brother. In Act II, scene ii, what we suspect is found to be true. There are two Constances, one the virtuous Northern lass and the other a Southern whore, Constance Holdup. The narrative resolution to the dilemmas now depends upon a succession of events affecting all three levels of the play—romantic, comic, and bawdy or farcical. Upon the advice of Tridewell, Mistress Fitchow agrees to give over any claims on Sir Philip if her brother is married to Constance, the Northern lass. A plot is laid so that Widgine is tricked into bed and a betrothal (in that order) with Constance Holdup disguised as the lass. As soon as she thinks she is free, Fitchow marries Tridewell and, finally, Philip is able to marry the Northern lass. Widgine manages to get out of an actual marriage to the whore by paying her off, but ultimately each gentleman gets what he desires and each lady (and I include the whore) what pleases her most.

Brome deserves credit, even at this early stage in his career, for his ingenious plotting of tightly integrated intrigues and counterintrigues into what Richard Levin calls "three-level drama"; plays which Levin says can be reduced to a formula: "a main plot consisting of characters deliberately elevated above the others, usually in heroic or romantic terms; a subplot of more ordinary people viewed from a more realistic and often ironic or satiric perspective; and a third group debased to the level of low comedy."[7] *The Northern Lass* comes the closest of Brome's three-level plays to fitting Levin's formula in that the serious romantic plot is the main one even though its activation depends on Tridewell and, perhaps because there is no social distinction between the serious and the comic plots, most of the satire is on the third, bawdy level.

Brome also shows talent for peopling his play with scintillating and varied characters. Clearly superimposed upon the multiple plots of the narrative structure and the romantic triangles of *The Northern Lass* are groups of character triads: the women— Constance, Fitchow, and Holdup; and the men—Sir Philip, Tridewell, and Widgine. Of the socially acceptable figures, Constance is the naive virgin whose sweetness of voice gives sound to her inner nature; Mistress Fitchow is also charming but experienced, shrewd with a city worldliness, and strident of tone. Each of the gentlemen is designed to be a fitting partner for his lady. Sir Philip, like his lass, is also somewhat impressionable and romantic in nature; Tridewell is more aggressive, like the widow also canny and sophisticated, and eminently capable of handling the testy Fitchow. Of particular interest, however, are Holdup and Widgine because they illustrate an art which Brome had for giving an original flair to characters usually presented as stock types.

The Southern whore, though integral to the earlier development of the play, does not appear on stage until Act IV, scene i. Already, however, she has been referred to as having "had a Bastard t'other day" (B 4^r; I,iv) and being a "prostituted strumpet" (E 3^r; II,iv), and it would be foolish to try to make her other than she is. Nonetheless, every attempt has been made to show Holdup as a sympathetic character. Although we first see her brought before the Justice for delinquency, this has already been established as part of Tridewell's plot and, amusingly, Vexham, the constable who charges her, emerges from the scene worse off than she does. The Justice's accusation against Vexham is a fine example of Brome's bawdy irony:

. . .It appears most plainly, that you think her to be one of the Trade, thought to make a Prey of her purse:[8] which since your affrightment,

could not make her open unto you, you thought to make her Innocence
smart for it. I will make your Knavery smart for it directly.

(H 3^v; IV,i)

After expelling Vexham to Newgate prison, however, Sir Paul
Squelch proceeds to proposition Holdup himself. Her explanation of her situation shows Brome's sympathy for Holdup and,
indeed, when Sir Paul remembers the misdeeds of her father
which led to her loss of station, he treats her as a lady, assigns her
a serving man, and provides ample funds for her personal needs
in return for her agreement to masquerade as the Northern lass.
In view of these circumstances, we have no need to doubt the
sincerity of Holdup's response to this treatment:

What shall I do with all this sir? I would need but an ounce or two of
thread, some knitting pins and Needles, and a Frame to flourish my
work on. Hereafter I will work in gold and silver, if you please, for your
wearing.

(I 1^v; IV,i)

But, as we find out two scenes later, she is privy to Tridewell's
plan to thwart Fitchow's attempt to betroth Widgine to the
Northern lass. Her soliloquy at the end of this sequence shows a
clear-sighted view of her own condition which cannot help but
engender some sympathy and understanding for the whore.
After she considers the dangers of being a part of the plotting,
she continues:

It brings likewise into my consideration, the baseness of my condition;
how much unpitied the punishment of a Whore is, and how suddenly it
overtakes her! My joint Conspirators are in no danger. I only run the
hazard, though they are as deep in fact as myself. Well, if I can scape
this pull, and draw any fortune by it, I'll change my function sure. A
common Whore? I'll be a Nun rather. . . .

(I 2^v-3^r; IV,iii)

Brome's characterization of the sort of woman usually ridiculed
and made the brunt of bawdy humor on the English stage is
somewhat like that found in *The Honest Whore Part I*. Indeed,
although Holdup does not become "new born" as Bellafront does
in the Dekker-Middleton play, nonetheless she maintains a
certain comic dignity in her willingness to forego her claim on

Widgine at the end of the play. In fact, unlike Bellafront, Holdup does *not* get stuck with a totally unsuitable match. Widgine, Mistress Fitchow's brother, is paired with Constance Holdup at the farcical, bawdy level of the play. Holdup, however, regardless of what else she might be, is no fool; Widgine, on the other hand, is just that. "Widgine," which means simpleton or ninny, indicates exactly what he is. Sir Philip no sooner meets his future brother-in-law than he begins to regret an obligation that would mix his blood "amongst a race of fools" (B 3ʳ; I,ii).⁹ Widgine is the prize gull of the play and much of the humor of the piece comes from his folly. Always good-humored, he remains convinced that his wit matches that of any of the others and that he is just as capable of intrigue. He is never more gleeful than when he reports to his sister the success of his masquerade as Sir Philip:

. . .The little Viper hung upon me, not to be shak'd off, 'til I promised her Marriage, and to father a Child, which, in her distraction, she conceited she had by me. I promised her anything; so took her into an inner room, to make all sure, as well within as without; and I so phillipt her —

(L 2ʳ; V,vi)

What he does not know, however, is that he has been wooing and bedding Holdup and not the Northern lass. Even when he does find out, his dismay is temporary. He quickly pays Holdup off and is his joyful, simple self again. It is just because Widgine is such a fool that Brome can use him as a vehicle for incidental but nonetheless incisive satire. The witless gullibility with which Widgine comments in absolute seriousness upon what constitutes a "gentleman" in contemporary London is a typical example of Bromean satire:

. . .A good man in the City is not called after his good deeds, but the known weight of his purse. One, whose name any Usurer can read without spectacles; One that can take up more with two fingers and a thumb upon the Exchange, than the great man at Court can lift with both hands; One that is good only in riches, and wears nothing rich about him but the Gout, or a thumb Ring with his Grandsire's sheepmark, or Grandam's butterprint on't, to seal bags, acquaintances and Counterpanes.

(D 2ʳ; II,i)

In addition to using what characters say and how they act to impress the audience with the individualities of their natures, Brome also employs song in *The Northern Lass* with an ingeniousness rarely shown by his contemporaries. The two Constances, for example, have five songs between them; three are sung by the lass and two by the whore masquerading as the unhappy virgin. Holdup's bawdiness provides dramatic counterpoint for the plaintive quality of the lass's love lyrics and *vice versa*. Brome, however, takes advantage of the similarities between the two girls as well as their differences; they have both, after all, been temporarily forgotten by Sir Philip in his pursuit of the wealthy widow. The fact that Holdup's sweetness of voice can pass for Constance's adds weight to the presentation of a girl as deserving of pity in her situation as the lass is in hers. Consider the two songs sung by Constance and Holdup in Act III, scene ii, and Act IV, scene iv, both of which are overheard by foolish suitors pretending to be Sir Philip. Each song has two parts with a rhymed couplet tucked into the dialogue separating the parts. In the first instance, when she is confronted by Master Nonsense, a silly Cornishman, the melancholy Constance sings of her despair at the absence of her love (G 2^r; III,ii) and then, as a total rejection of Nonsense, of her determination to remain a virgin unless she can have Sir Philip:

> *I wo' not go to it, nor I mun go to't,*
> *For love, nor yet for fee:*
> *For I am a Maid, and will be a Maid,*
> *And a good one till I die.*
> *Yet mine intent, I could repent, for ane man's company.*
>
> (G 4 ^{v}; III,ii)

Later Constance Holdup, masquerading as the Northern lass, comes to Widgine with her newborn child in her arms. She sings first of her despair at the absence of the child's father (I 3^v; IV,iv) and then completes her performance with a bawdy counterpoint to the Lass's pledge:

> *As I was gathering* April's *flowers*
> *He straight let fall one of his showers;*
> *Which drave me to an Arbour.*
> *Twere better I my Lap had filled*
> *Although the wet my clothes had spilled,*

> *Than to ha' found that harbour;*
> *For there a subtle Serpent was,*
> *Close lying, lurking in the Grass.*
>
> *And there while harmless thinking I,*
> *Still watching when the shower would die,*
> *Lay listening to a Bird,*
> *That singing sat upon the Bower,*
> *Her notes unto the falling shower*
> *The Snake beneath me stirred;*
> *And with his sting gave me a Clap,*
> *That swole my Belly not my Lap.*
>
> (I 4^{r-v}; IV,iv)

Both these songs are examples of Brome's skill in writing bawdy ditties. There is little doubt what either girl is singing about. However, comic fillip is added by couching the lass's pledge in the bluntest of terms and the whore's in paradisal metaphor. Holdup's delicacy of language also confirms for Widgine that this unfortunate maid is indeed the virgin he seeks.

The lass's second song,[10] *"Nor Love, nor Fate dare I accuse,"* is sung during a masque in Act II which purports to celebrate the wedding of Sir Philip to Mistress Fitchow. Although the evidence of dissension between the two has been shown before the masque, the mismatching is brought into sharp focus by Constance's presence. "It is a self-deprecatory song," says Professor Ingram. "Its pathetic appeal, combined with the gentle melancholy of the willow dance, causes Sir Philip to question his earlier rejection of Constance and to realize his hasty mistake in doing so."[11] The self-deprecation of the lass also contrasts with the haughty self-assertion of Mistress Fitchow, the comic member of the feminine triad.

Brome's presentation of Mistress Fitchow shows his skill in distinguishing the distinctive temperaments of his female characters by dramatizing their dissimilar reactions to similar situations—their being rejected by Sir Philip, for whatever reason. Already jealous because Philip has somewhat ingenuously confessed his love for the Northern lass, Fitchow is further piqued by the surprise announcement of the masque. Her voice, unlike the other women's, is obviously raucous because she threatens to "drown out their fiddling" should the masquers be allowed to enter. After a confrontation of wills between Fitchow

and Philip the performers enter, but "the fact that the masque is
allowed to go forward shows that Sir Philip has awakened to
Fitchow's contrariness [and] Constance's singing effectively
contrasts with Fitchow's sharp-temperedness. . . ."[12]
    Fitchow's other big scene comes in Act II, scene iii, signifi-
cantly placed between the lass's song on the absence of her lover
and Holdup's on the absence of her baby's father. Both
Constances, rendered helpless by rejection, sing sweetly of their
plight. Not so the widow Fitchow when she is "scorn'd and
revil'd." When even her servant and brother refuse to "succour"
her, she turns on Widgine like a fishwife. "What will become of
me? you Woodcock, Ninnyhammer." Widgine refuses to "med-
dle with another man's wife" and, in outrage, Fitchow flies at
him. All the others form a ring around Widgine and, while he
sings a mocking song about how to treat a nagging wife, *"she
scolds and strives to be amongst them"* (H 2ʳ-3ʳ; III, iii). We
might wish to protest the extent of Mistress Fitchow's ridicule
because she has been an unknowing participant in the romantic
dilemmas and, although the audience does not warm to her, she
is undeserving of such treatment. The scene, however, is a means
to an end. Tridewell's presence to comfort her with love and
understanding keeps us aware that, in addition to its significance
in developing the third feminine role, the sequence has a
valuable place in the total dramatic progression. It is integral to
Tridewell's plan for working out the romantic triangles at all
narrative levels.
    In *The Northern Lass,* the problems to be overcome by Philip
and Constance before their love can be sanctified in marriage
are of the hero's own making. Philip decides he is honor bound to
make good his promise to Fitchow even though he admits he
loves the Northern lass. Such a decision renders him impassive
and relegates the active role to the second hero, Tridewell. *The
Novella* and *The English Moor* also focus upon the maiden of the
title and how her lover wins her, but the barriers which stand in
the way are erected from the outside by what Northrop Frye
calls "obstructing figures"[13] and the social forces which they
represent. The romantic couples, although physically separated,
stand united against an alien although thoroughly comic world.
    Perhaps because Brome's lovers function within an identifi-
ably English world, this kind of confrontation makes room for
much more satire. At base the romances of Victoria (the novella)

and Millicent (the English moor) are still the narrative center of
these two plays, but the impact of the satire against the opposing
forces emerges in almost equal measure and, in turn, carries the
largest weight of Brome's moralizing. What results from these
plays is a Shakespearean or Fletcherian romance combined with
elements of the ironic mode, and the synthesis of these produces
something distinctively Bromean in style and moral expression.

II   The Novella

The Novella is a comedy of a Venetian society in which foreign
sources are adapted to contemporary English social custom.
Professor Kaufmann credits Richard Brome with a concerted
effort to capture the tone and mood of a Venetian love intrigue[14]
but the foreign setting of *The Novella* does not detract from the
play's essentially contemporary concern with the follies of
English society and with those issues which Brome consistently
lays open to ridicule and contempt. Robert B. Sharp says Brome
achieves a dramatic evolution from "a cynically realistic
anecdote" to "an idealistically romantic play of young love
triumphant over thwarting parents."[15] The characterization of
those "thwarting parents," however, Pantaloni (a doddering old
fool) and Guardagni (a miser or hoarder) and their servants
Nanulo (one of small or dwarfed wit) and Astutto (the cunning
one), remains realistic and varies little from when they are
mocked in other of Brome's plays in which their English names
are equally significant.

The plot conflict of *The Novella* centers upon the attempt of
two wealthy *senex* figures to force a marriage between their
respective children. It matters little to their fathers that Fabrito
is in love with Victoria, a poor lady supposedly residing in Rome,
and Flavia loves Francisco, an impoverished gentleman of
Venice. The two young men meet early in Act I and determine to
be each other's ally in thwarting the old men's plans. Further
extensions of exactly who loves whom (or what) are also included
in the first act. For one thing, Fabrito happens to see his father,
Pantaloni, sneaking through the darkness away from the area in
which new courtesan is lodged, a "Novella [who has] lately
come to Town." Night revelers who come upon the scene reveal
that this new addition is indeed a rare creature. Not only is she of
exceeding beauty but, as her name indicates, she is also an

apprentice to the craft of profligacy who is charging two thousand ducats for her virginity and a month of her company. "She is indeed," says one wry Venetian, "for beauty, Person, and Price, fit only for a Prince (H 6^{r-v}; I,i).

A fine speech at the beginning of Act I, scene ii, indicates clearly what it is Francisco's father, Guardagni, loves. Surrounded by his wealth and his account books, he salutes his possessions in words worthy of a Volpone:

> Whilest yet the Leaden finger'd god of sleep
> Keeps close the eye-lids of fantastic *youth*,
> Feeding their aery fancies with light dreams,
> Of wanton pleasures; giddy, vain delights,
> The ever watchful cares of aged Parents
> Throw ope the gates and shadows of soft rest,
> Making our midnight noon, to guard and order
> The wholesome fruits of our continual labour.
> Wholesome and happy off-springs of my pains
> Thus I salute you and implore your safety,
> And thus that you may rest, grow and increase,
> Mine eyes prevent the breakers of your peace.
>
> (H 7^{v}-8^{r}; I,ii)

The scenes which follow in rapid succession complete the pattern—Fabrito and Victoria love each other, Francisco and Flavia love each other, Pantaloni loves whoring, and Guardagni loves hoarding.

By the end of Act II, the circumstances and reasons for the disguises which will ultimately bring about the gulling of false and unnatural self-indulgence and the triumph of youthful natural love are firmly established. In the main plot, the novella is discovered to be Victoria, a revelation which does not surprise the audience. Her masquerade is to allow her social mobility through which she may seek out news of Fabrito; her high price is to protect her maidenhead. Fabrito borrows the robes of a hangman in order to inhibit his father's trick of revenge against the novella, who has outwitted the designs of her *vecchio inamorato* by a clever bed-trick. Later, when Fabrito realizes the novella is Victoria, the young lovers are reunited. In the other scheme, Francisco dresses up as a peddler-woman who brings a choice of wedding gifts to the prospective bride, Flavia. Once he is assured that Flavia is an unwilling marriage partner,

Francisco reveals his identity to her and the two elope.

If one of these intrigues can be said to be more serious, it is the plan to outwit Guardagni, in that it contains less of the comic mockery. Guardagni must share with Pantaloni Brome's disapproval of enforced marriage for selfish reasons whereas Pantaloni, because of his lustfulness and his vicious plot against Victoria (as well as his part in the enforcement), is trebly guilty of self-interest and deserves the major brunt of the satire. Thus, in narrative structure as well as in character interest, the comic level of the play is the main plot.

The novella is without doubt the cleverest participant in the comic confusion. Unlike the Northern lass, Victoria is in no way passive. She possesses all the ingenuity of a Rosalind and all the wit of a Viola. It is also important to recognize the skill with which Brome handles the virtuous heroine in her compromising position without her once offending the most delicate sensibility. The schemes and stratagems perpetrated in this play may be, as Professor Floyd suggests, "hardly respectable,"[16] but the purity and sensitivity of Victoria remain inviolate. In Act III, scene i, Victoria is approached by four men in succession, each convinced that he is the one who will possess the novella by dint of technique rather than by payment of the two thousand ducats. The bawdiness of the conversation apt for such a situation is deliberately directed to her "ruffiano."[17] In this way the dialogue is kept realistic while absenting it from the presence of Victoria. When Piso, a friend of Fabrito's, addresses her in crude phrases, she first responds that he obviously knows more about the ways of whores than she does and, when he persists, dismisses him:

> Sir, I must tell you now, you grow too lavish;
> So, as I fear foul language, to avoid which
> Let me entreat a fair departure hence.
>
> (K 3^r; III,i)

In the last act, Piso tries again to bandy suggestive words with her, and again her cool response cuts him short (M 1^r; V,i). Pantaloni's outraged question, "Are Bawds, and Whores Fit Matchmakers for Magnifico's Daughters?" is met with an equally terse retort, "Speak lower, or at home sir" (M 6^v; V,ii).

Unfortunately, Victoria remains the only fully developed and distinctive major character in the play. Flavia is little more than the conventional faithful damsel and the two young gentlemen are almost indistinguishable from each other. Jacquenetta's willingness to be a substitute bed-partner for Pantaloni in Act II, scene ii, opens the way for the kind of variety of character Holdup provides in *The Northern Lass,* but Brome uses her merely as a device here and again at the end of the play. The other secondary figures, although not without their comic moments, are also presented with little depth or individuality.

Victoria is the ultimate measure by which the antagonists to the successful fruition of natural love can be judged. Both fathers, Pantaloni and Guardagni, appear debauched when their morality is measured against that of the young lovers. As Professor Sedge has pointed out, Brome uses the very factor of the young people's forbearance from disobedience to underline his criticism of tyrannical parents[18]—and unnatural tyranny it is. The contrast is made all the more vivid by the ironic reversal provided by the novella. Here is a woman judged by society to be immoral; one who, by her service and the price for which she will provide that service, seems to personify both bodily and material self-indulgence but who is, in reality, virtuous and moral. Pantaloni and Guardagni, on the other hand, are esteemed by society as respectable magnificos with established legal authority on their side. Yet both are willing to sell their own flesh (in the persons of their children) for mercenary gain. Thus through ironic reversal, Brome extends the satire of *The Novella* beyond the mere ridiculing of foolish fathers to an attack on the pseudomorality of accepted social authority. And the results of the willing distortion of natural order by self-interest extends beyond the immediate follies of Venice. Through Piso, Brome makes quite clear his contention that when divine order is violated, the only result is chaos:

> Would you so Kick at heaven then, in despite
> Of its great Ordinance, so to force your children,
> To forfeit both their faiths, thereby to lose
> The never-failing hope of future blessings,
> To pull withall a curse on your own heads,
> That could no less than ruin your estates,
> And render you most wretched in your dotage,
> Past help or hope how to relieve yourselves:
> Your consciences still groaning underneath

The lashes of your Children's bastard issue
Should lay upon you?

(M 7^{r-v}; V,i)

The discord prophesied to be the result of the deliberate disordering of natural process is no less devastating within Brome's comic world than it is within Shakespeare's tragic one. Nonetheless, *The Novella* is a comedy, and in the dramatic conflict between fortune and nature, nature wins in the end. The "how" of the triumph of nature, however, creates a falling off in the final sequences of the play, a weakness in what is otherwise a more than competent stage representation. Although Victoria's purity is never questioned by the audience, others of her household are not so fortunate. Paulo, her "ruffiano," indulges in bawdy language and sexual innuendo that often lacks subtlety. So does her maid Jacquenetta, who has been Victoria's substitute in the bed-trick. But, in the last fifty lines of the play, Paulo turns out to be Victoria's brother who is a priest and Jacquenetta to be a "Eunuch moor" given her by Fabrito. These pander/priest, bawd/boy revelations maintain Victoria's social reputation but they are contrived and add two more disguises to a play already overburdened with mistaken identities. Despite Brome's skill in creating a distinctive heroine and his success in relating the various intrigues to a central theme of high moral tone, such unsuccessful dramatic devices cause the play to falter. The devices are not in themselves wrong; rather, the play is weakened by excess. Brome later uses the same techniques successfully but in *The Novella* too many tricks are needed to resolve the complications at the end of the play. Although deliberate doubling cuts down the number of characters on the stage at one time, the action tends to fragment. The levels of plotting, less perfectly executed than in *The Northern Lass*, are, as Swinburne has noted, "too exacting"[19] in their demands upon the audience.

The words are provided in the text for only one of the three songs called for in the stage directions and, if we can judge by this lyric, little care has been taken to integrate the auxiliary entertainments into the dramatic totality of the play. In fact, it is only with *The English Moor*, produced some four years later (1637), that Brome succeeds in presenting another dramatic vehicle as worthy of his skillfully drawn characters as was *The Northern Lass.*

III   The English Moor

Each of the three dramatic levels of *The English Moor* has its beginning in events previous to the stage action, receives its impetus in Act I, becomes increasingly complicated throughout Acts II, III, and IV, and, finally, is resolved into a satisfactory peace and harmony in Act V. In the order in which they are introduced to the audience one is serious, one satirically comic, and one farcical. As in *The Novella,* however, in hierarchal order of importance the three levels do not follow Levin's formula because the comic conflict that directly concerns Millicent, the English moor, is the center of dramatic attention. In fact, the serious plot demands least from the audience.

All three levels and their interconnections are quickly introduced to the audience in the first scenes. Prior to the opening of the play, Meanwell and Rashley, two gentlemen and friends, have quarreled and dueled, each supposedly killing the other. Dionisia, Meanwell's merciless daughter, insists that her brother Arthur seek "brave revenge" (A 3ᵛ; I,i) for their father's death by slaying Theophilis, Rashley's son. Arthur is thus faced with a mock-Romeo situation because he loves Lucy, sister to Theophilis. This moral antithesis forms the basis for the serious level of the play. Theophilis, the hero of the comic plot, is himself in love with Millicent, niece to old Testy but Millicent has been forced to marry Quicksands, a lecherous old usurer who has cozened every foolish young gallant in town. How she avoids being bedded by her aged spouse and is ultimately united with Theophilis provides the satirical action for the play.

To outwit Quicksands and Testy is not Millicent's only problem. Several young gallants, erstwhile friends of Theophilis, determine that they will seek revenge on Quicksands, the "bottomless devourer," by cuckolding him. Their plan, of course, threatens Millicent's honor; she must not only strive to keep out of Quicksands's bed but also keep the young men-about-town out of hers. This second problem and the subsequent action constitutes the farcical level of the play and through this further involvement of the heroine, the satirical and farcical levels of the play are linked.

In seeking to outwit the young men, Millicent has an ally. The leader of these young wantons, Nathaniel, has already been the "undoing of an honest maid" (A 5ʳ; I,ii), Phillis. Tricking Nathaniel into a permanent legal place in her bed is as important to Phillis as keeping him out of hers is to Millicent. Thus on the farcical level Nathaniel is as ripe for outwitting as Testy and Quicksands on the satirical level and Dionisia on the serious. In addition, linking the bawdy to the serious, is the willingness of the rascal-servant Ralph who spies for the single-purposed Dionisia in the hope she will reward him with lusty pleasures. Finally, the serious plot is connected to the comic when Dionisia, disguised to meet Theophilis, finds herself unable to hate him and, in fact, falls in love with the man she has sworn to be the object of her revenge. By a "domino" progression similar to that used in *The Northern Lass*, all three plot conflicts are solved. All three couples—Arthur and Lucy, Millicent and Theophilis, and Nathaniel and Phillis—are brought to the altar, but not before Brome has had an opportunity for dealing with three different motives for satiric attack—revenge, enforced marriage, and usury.

If there is a weakness in the plot structure of *The English Moor*, it again lies in Brome's penchant for relying on a *deus ex machina* for his resolution. Unlike the contrived revelation of previously unsuspected identities in *The Novella*, however, the reappearance of Meanwell and Rashley in the last act, with Phillis's father Winlose in tow, is almost to be expected. How else can revenge be resolved in a comedy except to remove the condition which motivated it? Unfortunately, why the two fathers plotted to deceive their children in the first place is left a mystery.[20] Rashley is only clear as to which purposes were *not* theirs, and to the suggestion that the mock duel might have led to a real one, he replies cynically:

> We had no fear of that, Sir, by the Rule,
> The common Rule o' the world. Where do you find
> Sons that have lives and Lands, will venture both
> For their dead Fathers that are gone and cared for?

This speech as it continues becomes a vehicle for Brome to attack the popular plot contrivances of lesser Caroline dramatists:

> Nor was it only to make a trial of
> What husbands they would be; how spend, or save;
> How manage, or destroy; how one or both
> Might play the Tyrants over their poor Tenants,
> Yet fall by Prodigality into the Compters:
> And then the dead by pulling off a Beard,
> After a little chiding and some whining,
> To set the living on their legs again,
> And take 'em into favour; pish, old play-plots.

$$(E\ 6^v-7^r;\ V,i)$$

More important, however, these charges are social satire, attacking contemporary conditions in London.

In the main action, Millicent keeps affairs well in hand, although Nathaniel and the other gallants who have been undone by Quicksands are unaware of it. Instead of protesting her innocence and virginity to the old roués when they try to hustle her off to her wedding sheets, Millicent takes on the role of a lusty wench. Her song shocks her new husband "quite out of Countenance":

> *She made him a bed of thistle down soft,*
> *She laid herself under to bear him aloft,*
> *And ever she sung sweet turn thee to me,*
> *We'll make the new bed cry Jiggy Joggy.*

$$(B\ 1^r;\ I,iii)$$

Insult is quickly added to injury for Quicksands when Millicent's songs are interrupted by a sow-gelders horn announcing the arrival of masquers. Herbert Allen has high praise for Brome's ability to "adapt masque. . .to give it a character in harmony with its surroundings," and, he says, its spirit "is sometimes one of broad comedy, almost a farce."[21]

Both masques—there are two in *The English Moor*—are vital to the development of comic action and theme. The first (B 2^{r-v}; I,iii), performed by Nathaniel and his followers, is skillfully adapted to the tone and circumstances of the scene. Its presenter, Mercury, describes an argument between Cupid and Hymen as to which might provide happier, "Love without

Marriage, or Marriage without Love." The contest between the two deities led to sad effects, for Hymen would not join the hands of those who loved and, instead, joined those whom his "new match-maker" brought before him. The masque, Mercury declares, is intended to show what sorrows lead from such "uncouth Policy." What might be called the Masque of Cuckolds follows, performed by a stag, a ram, a goat, and an ox, all with horns on their heads, and a courtier, a captain, a scholar, and a butcher. Each of the animals, explains Mercury, represents men who forced marriage on maidens for selfish reasons and, as a result, were cuckolded by the other characters. The last lines are obviously directed at Quicksands and the whole policy of enforced marriages:

> This is an Goatish Usurer, that must
> Needs buy a wretch's daughter to his lust;
> Doted, and married her without a groat,
> That Herald gave this crest unto his coat.
> . . . .
> Now by this dance let husband that doth wed
> Bride from her proper love to loathed bed
> Observe his fortune. . . .
>
> (B 2ᵛ; I,iii)

The laughter which this masque engenders stems from two main sources. There is the sequence itself with its combination of deities, humans, and animals gesticulating within the solemn framework of the stately masque; in addition, and quite in keeping with the theme of the play, is the condemnation of the marriage it supposedly honors presented in a form usually associated with celebration. Both the usual form and the usual purpose of the masque are set awry, resulting in comic and farcical reversals.

In terms of the plot, the masque also informs Millicent that others besides Quicksands "trench on" her virtue. In their determination to make the usurer cuckold, the gallants threaten her honor and a further plan becomes necessary to thwart the intentions of both husband and masquers. Millicent proposes that she stay with Quicksands for one month, locked up at night and disguised by day. Quicksands agrees, in order to trick the masquers, and suggests a disguise as a blackamoor, although, now

that he is assured of his bride's purity, he also plots to possess her
at the end of the time. Quicksands's painting of Millicent as a
moor, apart from its obvious parallel to his "black arts" of usury
and miserliness, symbolizes his attempt to entomb her within a
diabolic enforced marriage.[22] Testy agrees to the plan in hopes of
attaining Quicksands's money in payment for Millicent. As for
Millicent, she plays for time to seek a permanent solution to her
dilemma. The events which proceed from the plan provide the
narrative base for the quick-moving scenes of the next three acts.
Only at the end of Act IV do plots and counterplots come
together in another fine masque, this time of Quicksands's
devising.

Act IV, scene v, is a wonderful hoax. Everyone thinks he is
gulling someone else. Quicksands has previously announced the
death of Millicent but, in fact, plans to marry her at the end of
the masque, thus assuring himself of his wife and gulling those
who had ridiculed him for a cuckold. To a flourish of music, the
Inductor enters leading not Millicent, as Quicksands thinks, but
Phillis, the wench whom Nathaniel tried to discard, *"(black and)*
gorgeously decked with jewels." The Inductor explains that the
lady is the daughter of an Ethiopean queen who, if she marries a
white man, will become white. He then inspects each man's
hands before choosing Quicksands as the blackamoor's husband.
At this point the rest of the blackamoors enter and perform an
antimasque dance in which they mock and deride Nathaniel and
his friends.

Following the antimasque, Nathaniel asks permission to revel
with the black bride. While the others laugh at his suggestive
dance, he takes advantage of the opportunity for flirtation and,
under the cover of other jigs, dances Phillis to a couch off stage.
Although other complications not relevant to the masque follow,
what is important here is the double hoax. Quicksands is
horrified because he believes the blackamoor to be Millicent and
himself truly cuckolded; and Nathaniel, although at first only
interested in clapping a *"Barbary* buttock" (E 1r; IV,iv), is
delighted when he thinks he has done the act he originally hoped
for. This supposed situation is, of course, not true. Millicent is still
pure and, in the last scene of the play, after Quicksands has
demanded a divorce from the wife he thinks a whore, she is
returned to Theophilis. Nathaniel, on the other hand, thinking he
had aimed "at a cloud and clasped a Juno" (F 3r; V,iii), asks the

blackamoor to be his. Phillis is pleased to comply. Thus with the return of Meanwell and Rashley (contrived though it may be as a solution to the serious plot) and the double trickery provided by the second masque scene, all three levels of the play are brought to a happy and moral conclusion. The virtuous are rewarded and those who engaged in folly are brought to a sense of their own faults for the final scene of harmony and forgiveness.

All three feminine protagonists in *The English Moor* are given individuality and dramatic function. Lucy may be overshadowed by Dionisia, but her sensibility and compassion provide an effective foil for the latter's threatening influence. Although both girls believe they have lost their fathers, Dionisia's reaction to her loss is bitterness and severity, but Lucy advises Theophilis against hasty and irrational action.

Phillis is a more fully developed character than Lucy because her situation allows her greater freedom of movement and decision. Although it is not revealed until late in the play that she is the daughter of a respectable man who was, some six years hence, ruined "In a sad suit at Law" (E 7^r; V,i, a situation which allows Brome still another jab at unfair legal practices), Phillis is obviously not a mere comic servant girl seduced by a rake. Nor is she another Constance Holdup. It is clear in Act I, scene ii, that Nathaniel is the wanton one and that she has been indiscreet with him does not make her a bawd even though he brags he has taught her "a trade to live upon" (A 5^r; I,ii). She is certainly not without spirit, as Nathaniel finds out when he mocks her serving position, nor is she without enterprise, as he realizes after he has been tricked in the masque scene. Brome gives Phillis neither suggestive jibes nor bawdy songs (those go to Millicent to help her outwit Quicksands and Testy); rather he endows her with quiet perseverance and the determination to regain her honesty through marriage.

Richard H. Jefferson gives a prominent place to Dionisia in his study of *The English Moor* as a comedy of manners,[23] but the fact is, the play's interest centers on Millicent, one of Brome's finest heroines, and Dionisia, for all her vindictiveness, commands only passing interest. Millicent's faithfulness in her love for Theophilis and her verve and ingenuity in coping with encroachments on her honor combine the best qualities of the romantic Lucy and the realistic Phillis. Dionisia's function in the play is antiphonal; she exists as antilife and antimirth. Her negative strength is her weakness, her will is passive willfulness. Millicent, on the other hand, is positive, forthright, strong of will, and resourceful. Where Dionisia is static, Millicent is mobile; when Dionisia demands of others, Millicent guides her own destiny; Dionisia lacks wit and sensibility, Millicent is the epitome of them. Dionisia is the same antilife force in the serious plot as Quicksands and Testy are in the comic; her irrational desire for life-destroying revenge parallels Quicksands's life-destroying usury and Testy's insistence upon enforced marriage. In the farcical plot Nathaniel can be seen as antilife (although certainly not antimirth). His sexual energies are devoted to barren pleasures, as opposed to responsible procreation. Nathaniel is matched, however, with a fitting mate in Phillis and he accepts his comeuppance in good humor and with good grace. Thus, in each plot level of *The English Moor* attempts to sublimate positive life forces for revenge, for money, or for sexual irresponsibility are personified in particular characters who are ultimately brought into line by their opposite numbers who promote love, reason, and responsible human behavior.

The main impulse of each of these plays, *The Northern Lass*, *The Novella*, and *The English Moor*, has been romantic, and certainly an Elizabethan form of the romantic mode in their focus upon the heroines and in the basic conflict between natural impulse and contrived self-interest or nature versus fortune. Unlike the earlier writers of dramatic romances, however, Brome has chosen to identify his characters with the immediate and contemporary rather than the illusory or faraway and in so doing further transforms romance into a vehicle for carrying social and moral satire. These are not princes and princesses or pastoral aristocrats playing out games of courtly love in some remote green world. They are, nonetheless, lovers who overcome obstacles to their love with the same initiative and fortitude as their forebears, if not within the same genteel society. Brome's lovers function within a dramatic world peopled with misers and usurers, wenchers and whores, and witless gulls and wily servants; many of them are "humors" characters fashioned after the Jonsonian mold. Even so, when, as in *The English Moor*, romantic adventure remains in the foreground, when individual scenes peopled by idiosyncratic characters are fully exploited for their satiric worth, the total dramatic representation becomes a unified whole. In this way the play not only extols the encompassing virtues of romantic love but exposes the society which breeds individuals whose narrow self-interest brings about Brome's attack on human folly.

CHAPTER 3

The Gentlemen: Fathers, Fools, and Fops

I The Damoiselle

BY its title, *The Damoiselle* (1638) also appears to center upon the fortunes of a romantic heroine and, to an extent, the play is similar to those discussed earlier because the resolution of the narrative and dramatic movement hinges upon the disclosure of a gigantic hoax. Here, the final untangling of the complicated threads comes with the disclosure that Frances, the damoiselle, is not a maiden at all but the son of the melancholy Brookall whose loss of fortune and prestige triggers the dramatic action. *The Damoiselle,* however, is satiric rather than romantic, despite its concluding with no fewer than three romantic unions, not one of which is a bawdy postseduction match. Love intrigues are the structure upon which the plot is based, but the central themes of the play apply to the social and familial environment of the young people. Age is still wrong in its choice of values, and the attack against folly and vice is more pronounced, even though somewhat random. The initiative for righting wrongs and exposing follies falls to Sir Humphrey Dryground, described as a "decayed knight," who, by forcing atonement on others, is able to bring about his own expiation. Neither the title nor the subtitle, *The New Ordinary,* however, indicates that the movement is directed by an older man rather than a resourceful female. It is interesting to note that, with the increase of satire, the domination shifts from feminine characters to masculine. Indeed, all the plays to be discussed in this chapter, *The Damoiselle* (1638), *The City Wit* (c. 1629, rev. 1637–39), and *The Court Begger* (1640), are dominated by males.

The Damoiselle opens with the two main protagonists in

conversation over money. Dryground would borrow money from a parsimonious old usurer, Vermine, so that he might relieve the penury of Brookall, a victim of Vermine's vicious craft. Vermine, however, taunts Dryground about the motive for his charitable actions and the knight admits that a dozen years ago he was responsible for the seduction and desertion of Brookall's sister but adds how much he wishes he could "redeem that ruthful fault" (A 4^r; I,i). Vermine, as Dryground quickly points out, has the power to expiate his previous cruel inhumanities by allowing his daughter, Alice, to marry Brookall's son and giving her the inheritance which he cheated from the groom's father as a dowry. Vermine, of course, refuses. He has already made plans to advance his fortune further by marrying his daughter to Sir Amphilis, "a covetous Miser" (B 2^v; I,i).

In addition to laying the groundwork for the narrative, this scene introduces the first three father figures of the play: Brookall, Dryground, and Vermine. Brookall, we learn later, has been victimized first by Dryground, then by Vermine, and, finally, by the law of the land. He is almost totally passive throughout the entire dramatic action. From want of inheritance, Brookall's son has been forced out of society and, by disguising himself as the damoiselle, willingly becomes a part of Dryground's plan to outwit Vermine. Sir Humphrey Dryground, the director of the narrative action, is the most active father figure. In his determination to "redeem his fault," he is willing to become as decayed in fortune as he had been in moral honesty; the regaining of the second is much more important than the first. His son, Valentine, is the most admirable character of the play. He serves his father's plan but is in no way underhanded. Not having the taint of his father's earlier indiscretion, Val is able to work openly for the betterment and ultimate reconciliation of all the recalcitrant characters. The third father figure is Vermine, whose covetousness and lack of consideration for Brookall's desperate plight is such that it does not surprise us when he also considers his daughter merely a part of his goods. He has, prior to the action presented on stage, been very active; through his various questionable dealings, he has amassed a considerable fortune, arranged a profitable marriage for his daughter, and disowned his ne'er-do-well son. Once Dryground takes over, however, Vermine is helpless. He rants and raves and tries to scheme, but one by one the other characters, even his own son and daughter, join forces with Dryground against him. Vermine's family group makes up a triangle popular with Stuart dramatists—the usurer-rebellious daughter-prodigal son plot.[1] The combination of usurer with the perpetrator of enforced marriage makes Vermine doubly the villain of the piece, and the schemes to outwit him form the narrative action for the serious level of the play. Ultimately, he not only agrees to the marriage of Alice and Brookall's son but also to that of Wat, his repentant son, and Dryground's daughter whom the knight thought he had lost when he deserted her mother. Thus the three fathers, Brookall, Dryground, and Vermine, are all reunited with their children who, in turn, marry the mates of their choice, and the comedy ends happily.

In general, critics have not been particularly enthusiastic about *The Damoiselle*. Swinburne, although seeing "passages and scenes of genuine eloquence and of pathetic sincerity" in it, labels the play a "rough and wayward piece of dramatic composition or incomposition." "Indeed," he goes on, "if I mistake not, two or three better comedies might have been carved out of the material here compressed and contorted into the mold of one."[2] More recently Giles Floyd calls it "one of the author's least impressive efforts."[3] Still, both of these critics agree that the farcical level of the play gave to Caroline audiences one of Brome's finest and most original comic creations, Justice Bumpsey. He is, says Swinburne, "so fresh, and so genuine a sample of comic or farcical invention that Jonson might have applauded it with less extravagance or perversion of generosity than his cordial kindliness of nature led him sometimes to indulge in."[4] Bumpsey's distinction from the other father figures is clear: unlike Dryground, he has no title; unlike Brookall, he has maintained the fortune he has earned; and unlike Vermine, he has earned it respectably and legally. When the play opens, his daughter Jane is already married to Val. Although Bumpsey claims he might have married his daughter to a higher rank than Val is heir to, he will not interfere "were it *Ante Copulam,* as it is *post*" (B 4ᵛ; I,ii). He gives half of his fortune to Val; the other half he will keep himself and spend exactly as Val spends his share. Thus, if Val practices "good husbandry," he stands to gain at Bumpsey's death. Finally, unlike any of the other fathers, he manages to enjoy a great deal of fun from the situation he contrives and is the only one to give Sir Humphrey Dryground pause.[5]

Only R. J. Kaufmann has chosen to give almost unqualified approval to *The Damoiselle*. He finds the play strongly within the antiusury tradition and sees the entire play drawing its life from that. "Brome essays to put the issue of usury squarely in terms of brotherhood, that is, in terms of father-son, father-daughter, man-to-man relationships and to make clear that goods cannot rightly take priority over the bonds of love."[6] Kaufmann sees the play as an eminently serious one and even goes so far as to say "though the play is called a comedy, it is what the twentieth century would call simply a drama."[7] In fact, however, it is only when Brome allows the seriousness to dominate the stage that the play falters into invective and sentimentality. Brookall's mournful diatribes against Vermine are tedious and excessive. If the audience does not already know the seriousness of Vermine's denials of love and humanity by the time this poor creature takes the stage, the playwright has wasted almost all of the first two acts. Although Kaufmann does allow that Bumpsey provides a counterbalance to Vermine's vicious outlook on money and children, he neglects Bumpsey's equally important dramatic function as comic commentator on the issues of the play. It is Bumpsey who exposes false superiority and he does it with a certain comic dignity. When the "decayed knight," Dryground, meets citizen Bumpsey, it is the knight who comes off badly. Bumpsey, in his garrulous way, brags that his daughter could have made a better match than with young Valentine; but Dryground points out that such a match might not have been to a "gentleman." The Justice's quick reply completely undercuts the knight:

> Yet honourable, Land-Lordship's real honour,
> Though in a Trades-man Son: when your fair Titles
> Are but the shadows of your Ancestry:
> And you walk in 'em, when your land is gone:
> Like the pale Ghosts of dead Nobility.

Although the knight tries to interrupt, Bumpsey goes on:

> Your son (I say) is Heir to your bought honour.
> Which may hereafter Ladify my Daughter:
> But where's the Land you once were Lord of? Ha!

The goodly Cornfields, Meadows, Woods, and Pastures?
. . . .
You, that had all these once, in three fair Lordships,
To be wrought on, and toneyed out of all,[8]
But a small pittance of *Trois Cents per Annum*,
By Providence entailed upon the Heir,
(Or that had wasted too) which now maintains you.
. . . .
Can you (I say) think your good husbandry
A lawful Precedent for your Gamesome son
To make my Daughter happy in Marriage,
Though he had twice my Fortunes?

                                        (B 4^v-5^r; I,ii)

Foolish prattler though he may be, Bumpsey continually shows himself to be a man with a fine realistic sense of values, a perspective which the other father figures lack. Professor Sedge gives credit to Brome for the subtlety and skill of his didacticism in this sequence:

Although Bumpsey is gently satirised as he preaches this sermon. . .yet the point hits home. Brome's characterisation of Bumpsey as taking delight in this opportunity for a self-righteous vindication of his thrift at the expense of the knight. . .does not invalidate his lesson that wealth deserves social respect. By dramatising the issue in terms of character Brome avoids simplification into abstract sociological terms and at the same time achieves something more than flat didacticism.[9]

By dramatizing social issues through character confrontation, Brome is able to expand the scope of his satire to include *any* false sense of values. In Act III, scene ii, old Vermine takes his turn as victim of Bumpsey's sermonizing. The usurer has approached the Justice for advice and comfort in the loss of his daughter and, again, Bumpsey's words make dramatic still other issues of the play.

Shall I be plain wi' ye [says Bumpsey];
My best advice is, since your Daughter's gone,
To turn your Son after her. He lies not in
For much above a hundred pound. Pay it,
And let him take his course: If he be not
Got loose already. Then (observe my Counsel)
Spend you the rest of your Estate yourself;

And save your Heirs the sin. It is the course
'I have in hand, and mean to follow it.
You like it not (it seems) but thus it is,
When men advise for nothing. Had your Lawyer
Now for his fee, given Counsel, might have damned you:
You would have thought it worth your Gold, and follow'd it.

(D 7ᵛ; III,ii)

Vermine's miserliness and greed have given rise to the sins of his
own heirs and, in a serious sense, his son Wat is his father's
punishment. Wat is the living example of the very prodigality
upon which Vermine has preyed in other men. In addition to the
actual meaning of Bumpsey's advice, however, the Justice
succeeds (where, up to this point, Dryground has failed) in
making Vermine look ridiculous. Vermine undergoes a conversion at the end of the play, and some basis must be provided for
the credibility of that conversion. Bumpsey provides it by
lightening Vermine's villainy, at least briefly, by making him
appear more foolish than the Justice is garrulous. Jane's comment
on the action at this point is that "the World is turn'd Quite
upside down" (D 8ʳ; III,ii) and this is exactly what Bumpsey is
able to do—turn the action upside down. The citizen instructs
the aristocrat; the comic makes the villain think he is addled; the
Justice proves the falseness of the law.

This last is a much less clearly defined function for Bumpsey
but is nonetheless there. The law or man-made statute comes off
very badly in this play; "that Law," as Brookall laments:

once called sacred, and ordained
For safety and relief to innocence,
Should live to be accursed in her succession,
And now be styled Supportress of oppression;
Ruin of Families, past the bloody rage
Of Rape or Murder: all the crying sins
Negotiating for Hell in her wild practice.

(C 5ᵛ; II,i)

Brookall refers to the law which charges fees for counsel that
damns personified in the Attorney who would buy an oath from
Brookall, in the lawyers who are continually crossing the stage
engaged in diabolical plans by which they will be "swollen
bigger" by the emptiness of those they have contrived to gull and

cheat (E 4ʳ; IV,i), and in the Sergeants who admit their "Office"
is as honest as a "bawdy-house" (F 7ʳ; V,i). This law is directly
antithetical to natural moral law, which teaches honesty, love,
and humanity as they are dictated through conscience. The
various intrigues which bring about the triumph of moral law are,
of course, under the direction of Sir Humphrey Dryground, but
at the end of the play, when Vermine would still deny his
blessing to his restored daughter, it is Bumpsey whose words
pinpoint the necessity for him to turn to moral law for guidance:

Shall I tell you Neighbour? Law has no relief for you; And Conscience
and you have a long time been strangers. Could you be friends and
embrace Conscience now, all would be well. And there's the substance.
Is it plain?

(G 2ʳ; V,i)

And indeed it is plain. Vermine embraces both his daughter and
his reformed son, agrees to their marriages, and the play is over.
Under the moral guidance of Bumpsey, natural love, parental
and romantic, triumphs over selfishness and greed.

II   The City Wit

In *The City Wit* (c. 1629; rev. 1637–39), one of Brome's best
social satires, the London citizen is again presented with good
humor and sympathy and allowed to be the instructor of sound
moral principles. Unlike in *The Damoiselle,* however, the leading
character who directs the actions and intrigues is at once a
"young Citizen fallen into decay" and the voice of bourgeois
morality. Crasie thus assimilates the narrative function of
Dryground and the thematic function of Bumpsey into one
character.

Similarities between *The City Wit* and *The Damoiselle* (and
also *The Court Begger,* which followed in 1640) suggest that the
play was not only revived by the author in the late 1630s but also
revised.[10] The basic plot bears ample evidence of Jonson's
influence, even if the author had not acknowledged it in the
Prologue, but it also shows those unmistakable characteristics of
Bromean plot manipulations and high morality. Like *The
Alchemist, The City Wit* is structured upon a series of gullings or

outwittings. In the Brome play, however, Crasie, who has learned the lesson of excessive generosity to unreliable friends, is determined to regain that which was his and at the same time to teach a lesson in the responsibilities of love, friendship, and brotherhood. Crasie, his apprentice Jeremy (disguised as Mistress Tryman), and Crack, a servant boy, form a triumvirate of conspirators which Crack describes as "By Indenture Tripartite, and't please you, like *Subtle, Doll,* and *Face.*" His song pledges their mutual advantage:

> *Then let us be friends, and most rarely agree.*
> *The Pimp and the Punk and the Doctor are three,*
> *That cannot but thrive, when united they be.*
> *The Pimp brings in custom, the Punk she gets treasure.*
> *Of which the Physician is sure of his measure,*
> *For work that she makes him in sale of her pleasure.*
> *For which, when she fails by diseases or pain,*
> *The Doctor new Vamps and upsets her again.*
>
> (C 7ᵛ-8ʳ; III,i)

Rather than being just another "coney-catching" drama, however, *The City Wit* is more within the tradition of the moralities; in addition to mocking the wayward, it also brings the erring to judgment and reform.

The play has obvious similarities to *Volpone* and to *Epicoene*. Mistress Tryman's illness is, like Volpone's, designed to trap legacy-hunters; the discovery that the lady is really a male accomplice to the outwitter is akin to Epicoene's disguise as the silent woman. Through ingenious plotting and skillful depiction of character, Brome is able to expose the follies and vices of the city. Although he appears to present the irony of honesty paying off only when dishonest means are employed to bring it about, the play actually demonstrates that dishonesty is mere "virtuosity in deception," whereas "honesty and fair dealing" are the outgrowth of "an attitude superior to mere skill in achieving economic success."[11]

Crasie is an interesting variant on the usual stage prodigal in that his "decay" has been brought about by bankrupting himself for his so-called friends. As the play opens, his creditors are hounding him for payment but his debtors are nowhere to be found. Recognizing his situation as desperate, he determines:

I must take nimble hold upon Occasion,
Or lie forever in a Bankrupt ditch,
Where no man lends a hand to draw one out.
I will leap over it, or fall bravely in it,
Scorning the Bridge of Baseness, Composition,[12]
That doth infect a City like a Plague,
And teach men Knavery, that were never born to it:
Whereby the Rope-deserving Rascal gains
Purple and Furs, Trappings and golden Chains.
Base Composition, baser far than Want,
Than Beggery, Imprisonment, Slavery:
I scorn thee. . . .

(A 5^{r-v}; I,i)

Having set his course firmly, he then proceeds through a series of disguises to cozen two courtiers, a pedant, "a thrifty citizen," his mother-in-law, his brother-in-law, and his own wife into returning to him things they had either borrowed or stolen. At first each is dealt with individually and then one is set upon the other in a series of counterintrigues whereby each is led to comeuppance through manifestations of his own greed and foolish social speculations. With the aid of Mistress Tryman and Crack, Crasie plays upon the self-interest of each so that they turn on one another and bring about defeat for themselves and victory for Crasie.

Of the various gulled characters, Mistress Pyannet Sneakup, Crasie's mother-in-law, is Brome's most distinctive character creation of the play and the one through whom most of the direct satire against human misconceptions is generated. She is totally unsympathetic to the kind of generous dealing that has led Crasie to ruin; she worships rank and money and will go to any lengths to find a suitable mate for her dimwitted son; she is a loquacious shrew, an indiscriminate lecher, and a ruthless social climber.[13] Obviously, Pyannet is designed to represent Crasie's antithesis. While he voices generous human dealings, she voices the self-oriented dogma of the city climber who, though comic, can be vicious. When Crasie tries to explain his attitude toward honesty and trust to his henpecked father-in-law, Pyannet will not let him get a word in edgewise.

Honest man! [she shrills,] Who the Devil wished thee to be an honest man? . . . Honesty! What should the City do with honesty; when 'tis enough to undo a whole Corporation? Why are your Wares gummed; your Shops dark; your Prizes writ in strange Characters? what, for honesty? Honesty? why is hard wax called Merchants' wax; and is said seldom or never to be ripped off, but it plucks the skin of a Lordship with it? what! for honesty? . . . Did we marry our Daughter, here, to thee; racked our Purses to pay Portion; left Country housekeeping to save charges, in hope either of thine, or her honesty? No, we looked, that thy Warehouse should have eaten up Castles, and that for thy narrow Walk in a Jeweller's shop, a whole Country should not have sufficed thee.

(A 6^v-7^r; I,i)

The difference between Crasie and his mother-in-law is clear—one is a healthy contributor to the human state and the other, the "maggot-pie," an unhealthy parasite destroying the host upon which she presently feeds. All the other gulls are also, in varying degrees, parasites; even Josina, Crasie's wife, follows in her mother's footsteps and admits stealing two jewels from her husband. Her claim at the end of the play that she knew her husband even through his disguise is not very convincing. Nevertheless, Crasie accepts her expression of innocence; no one knows better than he that whatever her inclination may have been, Josina had no chance to be false. We might question whether Josina's bawdiness may be seen as coarse catering to the audience, but if this were one of Brome's intentions it was not his only one. Josina's self-indulgence provides a variation from those who seek social position and economic gain; moreover, considering Pyannet is already the garrulous shrew, we might ask what else Josina could have been but the wayward wife.

As for the others, Ticket and Rufflit (two "professed" courtiers) and Lady Ticket use their small position to prey upon those who would desire social advancement. Ticket's response to Crasie's honest request for repayment of a loan is indicative of their lack of moral fiber and of Brome's attitude toward court hangers-on:

. . . Dost take me for a Citizen, that thou thinkest I'll keep my day? No, thou'st find that I am a Courtier, let my day keep me and 'twill. But dost hear? Come to the Court. I owe the two hundred pounds: I'll not deny

it, if thou ask seven years hence for it, farewell. I say no more, but come
to Court, and see if I will know thee.

(B 1ᵛ; I,ii)

Although the contrast between the citizens' and the courtiers'
attitudes toward debt is favorable to the merchant class, Brome
does not let all tradesmen escape his attack. Linsey Wolsey, the
miserly draper, comes in for his share of Bromean satire.
Sometime previously, Linsey Wolsey had secured from Crasie a
jewel worth sixty pounds to be repaid on the draper's wedding
day. In the meantime he has sold the jewel for thirty pounds.
Now, because of his financial straits, Crasie is willing to settle for
twenty. Linsey Wolsey's offer is reprehensible and is tantamount
to usury, a practice particularly deplored by Brome:

. . . If twenty pound will pleasure you, upon good security I will
procure it you. A hundred if you please, do you mark Mr. *Crasie?* On
good security. Otherwise you must pardon me, Mr. *Crasie.* I am a poor
Tradesman Mr. *Crasie,* keep both a Linen and a Woolen Drapers' shop,
Mr. *Crasie,* according to my name, Mr. *Crasie,* and would be loath to
lend my money, Mr. *Crasie,* to be laughed at among my Neighbors, Mr.
Crasie, as you are Mr. *Crasie.* And so fare you well, Mr. *Crasie.*

(B 3ʳ; I,ii)

Sarpego, the foolish pedant whose ambition is to be tutor to
the prince, in spite of the distasteful quality of his name, is the
least insidious and most purely comic of the parasites. There is
not even anything monumental about his debt to Crasie; it is only
a "driblet" lent out of the merchant's purse. Yet he is a fine
character device for some of Brome's most subtle ironies. When
Crasie asks Sarpego for the money owed, the pedant replies in a
circumlocution involving a question which he claims was asked of
Tacitus by Diogenes Laertius at the end of which Sarpego
refuses payment and gives a fatuous benediction:

. . . Well Sir, I shall ever live to wish, that your own lantern may be
your direction; and that, wherever you travel, the *Cornu copia* of
Abundance may accompany you. . . .

(B 2ʳ; I,ii)

The lantern reference identifies the Diogenes to which Sarpego
refers as the Greek philosopher (c. 412–323 B.C.) who went forth

searching for an honest man. This is not, however, the Diogenes
Laertius who was a recorder of philosophical comment living in
the early third century. Thus the speech allows the ironic thrust
that this man should prate to Crasie about a search for an honest
man while at the same time revealing the falseness of his
pedantry. Still another subtlety is apparent in the word *lantern*,[14]
which, when coupled with the separation of *Cornu* from *copia*
and Sarpego's unwitting substitution of "plenty of horn" for
"horn of plenty" becomes so obviously an obscene joke that even
the most unlearned member of the audience would understand.
Finally the audience is prepared early in the play for what to
expect every time Sarpego spouts his pseudoerudition. In fact,
such early audience preparation should appease Professor
Ronald Bayne's concern over how much of Sarpego's comical
Latin was followed by the audience.[15] Throughout the play
Sarpego converts, willingly if unwittingly, various Latin phrases
into comic paraphrase. Some of these are so obvious that any
schoolboy would see the humor: *Sic transit gloria mundi* (Thus
passes the glory of the world) becomes "The learned is coney-
caught" (D 6^r; III,vi); for *Elephantem ex Musca facit* (She makes
an elephant out of a fly), the first phrase used by Erasmus to
describe the Sophists of Greece, Sarpego substitutes the second,
"She takes me for a mountain that am but a Mole-hill" (D 8^r;
IV,i). Once having realized the kind of humor being used, the
audience would laugh from the very impetus of comic repetition
whether or not it actually understood every Latin phrase.

A very un-Jonson-like part of *The City Wit* is the masque
provided in Act V for the marriage of Tobias Sneakup and
Mistress Tryman. Jonson so abhorred the mixing of entertainment forms that it would not be unreasonable to suggest that the
masque was not a part of the original play but added by the
younger playwright in the later revisions. If this be the case, the
addition is a fine example of Brome's developing skill in handling
the masque form as a device for both comic irony and dramatic
resolution.

It is not at all out of character that Mistress Pyannet Sneakup
should be the one to demand a masque for her son's wedding in
spite of the apparently grave illness of the bride for masque was
an aristocratic entertainment and Pyannet now feels assured of
her advanced social position. For the audience, the whole
performance is predetermined to be farce, and Brome does not

let his viewers down. Sarpego is to be producer, casting director, and inductor for the entertainment which, he says, will take the form of a learned ballet "full of nothing but moral conceits betwixt Lady *Luxury*, a Prodigal and a Fool" (F 6ᵛ; V,i). Tryman and Crasie, however, have been working behind the scenes and Crack's nuptial song turns out to be another of the bawdy ditties at which Brome is so successful; Tryman turns the tables on Tobias and plays the Billingsgate whore with a vengeance; and, when Crasie finally appears, he is not in the image of the Prodigal Son but rather the lavish display of Prodigality. He is *"in his own habit, all hung with Chains, Jewels, Bags of Money, &c."* (G 1ʳ; V,i). He has gained back much more than he had previously lost through his generosity to his false friends and relatives. His surprise entry is followed by the general unmasking of the self-centered interests of the various parasites and, although there are no final revels to end the masque, there is a general reconciliation and the promise of a "merry night."

III   The Court Begger

The City Wit is one of Brome's best London social satires. Its episodes are held together by the central character of Crasie and by the dramatized folly of self-advancement through immoral means. *The Court Begger* (1639–40), on the other hand, is a political satire in which Brome shifts his attack away from individual types and focuses on the whole system of preferment, position, and monopoly as it was practiced in and around the Caroline court. Although Brome uses individual and recogniz-able public figures to intensify his protest—an indulgence rarely found elsewhere in his work—and although he again uses a romantic frame in which enforced marriage is condemned, *The Court Begger* is a political satire in which the ethic of unmerited advancement and irresponsible favoritism is attacked.

Like the other plays discussed to this point, the action of *The Court Begger* centers upon the figure of the title, in this case Sir Andrew Mendicant, "an old Knight, turned a projector." As indicated by his name, the foolish old man has become little more than a beggar. The conversation with his niece in the opening scene reveals that he has lost everything through various bubblelike schemes to advance himself at court and he is now placed in the position of begging for favors from Sir

Ferdinand by using his niece Charissa as bait. That she loves the poor young Frederick or that Ferdinand is thought to be distracted with love for Lady Strangelove, a wealthy widow, means nothing to Mendicant. He insists upon forcing a marriage which will be to his advantage regardless of the dispositions of his niece or anyone else. The main plot, then, is concerned with the folly and ultimate defeat of Mendicant's striving for court position and influence and with the exposure of a vicious system which allows total disregard of personal feeling or moral ethic. A second focus of interest lies in the strange entourage of Lady Strangelove, a group of self-seeking fops aptly named Courtwit, Citwit, Swaynwit, and Dainty. Such a group allows Brome to intensify his attack on the system by showing the number and types of people involved in it. Finally, subordinate to these, though nonetheless important in providing plot impetus, are the romantic entanglements involving Frederick, Charissa, Ferdinand, and Lady Strangelove. The words of the young romantic lover pinpoint Brome's attack on the whole process of court preferment. When Frederick finds out that Ferdinand's intents toward Charissa are dishonorable, he charges that the knight is not a true Courtier but

> A mere vainglorious imposture;
> Pretending favour, having nothing less.
> Witness his want of Merit. Merit only
> It is that smoothes the brow of Majesty,
> And takes the comfort of those precious beauties
> That shine from grace Divine: and he's a Traitor
> (No way to stand a courtier) that to feed
> His Lusts, and Riots, works out of his Subjects
> The means, by forging grants of the King's favour.
>
> (Q 6^r; IV,i)

Professor Kaufmann has identified the character of Sir Ferdinand as Sir John Suckling, and he is no doubt right. "Suckling," he says, "epitomized just those Cavalier qualities which Brome reprehended." Kaufmann also proves that Court-wit is a direct satire on Sir William Davenant,[16] for Brome's reprehension "was extended to the professional dramatist, Sir William Davenant, who increasingly identified himself with Suckling and the court circle while he pushed forward his considerable ambitions for a professional theater under his own management."[17] Professor Sedge agrees. "Brome equates," Sedge says, "the system of court preferment which ignores wider considerations of social desert with the attempts of dramatists like Davenant and Suckling to make drama a dilettante pursuit for a small elite. The amateur playwright who scorns apprenticeship to the trade is analogous to the favourite who takes short cuts to reach social distinction."[18]

Still another identification is that of Dainty, "a supposed Picturedrawer, but a Pick-pocket," as Inigo Jones. The actual connection of Jones with Davenant was more than a casual court acquaintanceship. Jones had designed the scenery for Davenant's masque *The Temple of Love* which had been produced on Shrove Tuesday 1634, a time when Ben Jonson's loss of court favor was felt acutely by those who sided with the old laureate. Again, in 1637, Davenant and Jones came together as copresenters of *Britannia Triumphans*. After Jonson's death and Davenant's appointment to succeed him as laureate, Jones was designer for a Davenant masque, *Salmacida Spolia*, produced in January 1640. When Lady Strangelove commissions Courtwit (Davenant) to be responsible for the "poetical part" of a masque which she wishes to be presented, the obvious identification for the audience of Dainty who was to fulfill "the Painter's office for the scene," would be Inigo Jones. As Courtwit has a "project" to restrict the plays to be admitted to the stage and to instruct all the actors in the city, so Dainty has his:

Sir I am a Picture-drawer Limner, or Painter (if you please) and would gladly purchase authority, by myself and deputies, for the painting of all the Kings' and Queens' '-head signs for Taverns, Inns, Ale houses, and all Houses and Shops of Trade throughout the Kingdom upon this ground that they draw and hang up their royal Images for signs in so hideous manner that men bless themselves to see it.

(P 4ᵛ; II,i)

That Dainty (Inigo Jones) is a pickpocket implies that the designer lives out of the pockets of stage artists. This becomes doubly ironic when he even picks the pocket of Courtwit (Davenant) himself. In the Prologue to *The Court Begger* Brome makes clear his disapproval of Cavalier drama and expresses his own allegiances; he appears to include Jones in his attack upon contemporary practices by his reference to the "gaudy scene" which lesser dramatists rely upon to please their audiences.

Finally, in the masque at the end of the play, the whole satiric enterprise of the play comes together. By the time Act V opens, Sir Ferdinand's feigned madness has been exposed, and he has agreed to help Lady Strangelove and Frederick in their plot to outwit Mendicant. Then, in Act V, scene i, Dainty is forced to confess he is a thief. "The Kings Picture-drawer?" comments Citwit, "A neat denomination for a Cut-purse, that draws the King's Pictures out of men's Pockets" (R 8ᵛ; V,ii). The coupling of Charissa and Frederick, the conversion of Sir Andrew Mendicant, and the expulsion of the projectors bring the action to its typical Bromean ending in reconciliation and harmony.

The first takes place almost immediately in Act V, scene ii. In bridal procession, Charissa is led across stage past her father, who blesses her in what he thinks will be her marriage to Ferdinand. This procession begins an extended masque sequence in which real purposes and identities are hidden behind the facade offered by the courtly entertainment. On stage, the preparation for the masque acts as a cover for the real marriage of Charissa and Frederick—Courtwit mumbles and composes, the doctor sings, Citwit dances, Philomel recites classical lines, Dainty plays the viol. All the masque elements are there, except they are jumbled up in rehearsal and, as such, constitute the first antimasque. The narrative link between this antimasque and the masque proper is provided by the public exposure of Mendicant's foolishness. Further, the self-entanglement which has resulted from Mendicant's schemes allows Brome to bring home still another satiric thrust—an attack against the granting or selling of confiscated estates and legal guardianships. Mendicant had been "begging" for royal court favors and monopolies through "Mediators tongues" (N 7ᵛff; I,i) besides his begging through the legal courts. Thus the title of the play takes on a dual meaning. The statute establishing the Court of King's Wards (1540) which declared that the estates of minors, idiots, and heiresses under the King's wardship should be transferred to the jurisdiction of this Court, also allowed the officers of the Court of Wards to grant or sell these wardships.[19] Under this law Mendicant had "begged" the estate of Ferdinand, whom he thought addled (O 2ᵛ; I,i). Having taken advantage of this iniquitous custom of "begging," it is only fitting that he be caught up in the same system. Earlier, in a fit of temper, Sir Mendicant had wounded his servant for daring to act as a cover for Charissa and Frederick. Now, Mendicant is informed by Sir Ralph, a would-be-wise, that the lad is dying. Although the projector's culpability in the offense is obvious, "as 'twas done in the heat of blood," he may get off with his life. As a felon, however, Mendicant's goods and chattles should be forfeit and up for begging (S 4ᵛ; V,ii), but he is offered an alternative: Sir Ralph will remit the estate if Mendicant will agree to the marriage of Charissa and Frederick. When Mendicant protests that Frederick is dead, Lady Strangelove ushers in the newlyweds. Ferdinand's demand for the return of his estate which Mendicant had begged brings all Mendicant's speculations tumbling about him. The tables are turned when the little he has left is begged for manslaughter. His moans of self-pity quickly change to anger when his servant appears hale and hearty and, willfully, he storms off stage as the revelers for the masque enter. " 'Tis all but show," he protests, "let go, and I will do Something shall add to your delight immediately" (S 5ʳ; V,ii).

Although the concluding comic sequence lacks the high style of a regular Court Masque, the ordered structure of the entertainment still represents the same reestablishment and affirmation of moral values demanded of a Jonson masque. Brief though it may appear in the text, the sequence is complete and, more important, successfully integrated into the total stage performance. Earlier, there had been a stage procession and the first antimasque; now the allegorical figures, played by characters from the play proper, take the stage.

The purpose and intent of the masque is presented in a conversation between Venus and Cupid. Hymen, Venus explains, has done his office too "faintly" here and, to remedy the situation, she has summoned the "Champions for the Queen of Love." These are

> *Courage* [Swaynwit], sent from *Mars; The Muses' [s]kill*
> [Courtwit]
> From wise *Apollo.* And the God, which still
> Inspires with subtlety, sly *Mercury*
> Sends this his *Agent* [Dainty]. Here's *Activity* [Citwit]
> From *Jupiter* himself; And from her store
> Of Spies, the Moon sends *This* [Doctor][20] to keep the door,

and their charge is

> With Art of Action, now, make good the place,
> In right of Love to give the Nuptials Grace.
>
> (S 5ᵛ; V,ii)

As the masquers dance their measures, they are interrupted by an antimasque of projectors who reveal dolefully that Mendicant has gone mad and hanged himself. Hanged himself, that is,

> All over sir, with draughts of Projects, Suits,
> Petitions, Grants, and Patents, such as were
> The Studies and the Labours of his Life,
> And so attired he thinks himself well armed
> T' encounter all your scorns.
>
> (S 6ʳ; V,ii)

Mendicant, *"attired all in Patents"* with a windmill on his head, enters and calls for room for the "Monopolist" to declare his wares. The regular masquers protest, however, and in a wild antimasque dance they pull off his patents and the cloaks of his projectors, whom they quickly thrust off stage. Ferdinand's cry, "An excellent Moral! The Projects are all cancelled, and the Projectors turned out of doors," indicates that Mendicant is finally cured. An exchange of faith between Ferdinand and Lady Strangelove ties up the last threads of the narrative action and the masquers dance the final measures before the company sweeps off stage for a nuptial supper. Thus the masque and the play come to an end.

Although we might question Swinburne's linking of *The Court Begger* with *The City Wit* as "twin comedies of coarse-grained humour and complicated intrigue [in which] we breathe again the grimier air of Cockney trickery and Cockney debauchery," we cannot but agree that the satire in these plays "is even now as amusing as it is creditable to the author to have seconded. . .the noble satirical enterprise of Massinger and Ben Jonson against the most pernicious abuses of their time."[21] If *The City Wit* and *The Court Begger* may be compared, the reason for doing so would not be because the plays are both lowbrow (which *The Court Begger* is certainly not), but rather because in spite of the episodic structure which would classify them as farces, the satiric thrust is as skillfully concentrated as in the best plays of any of Brome's more famous contemporaries. Felix E. Schelling is specific on this point in his praise for *The Court Begger*. It turns, he says, "with kaleidoscopic effect [upon] the familiar figures of separated lovers, angry father, scheming widow, and attendant gulls, with the variation of a group of 'projectors' conceived and executed with a spirit that the creator of 'the ladies collegiate' or 'the staple of news' might not have disdained."[22] Unlike *The Damoiselle*, in which the attack strikes out diffusely at various targets in its many episodes, the two later plays explore different aspects of the same moral turpitude—opportunism sanctioned by political irresponsibility. The insistence that aristocracy lies in nature and not in fortune is as much a distinctively Elizabethan tenet as it is conspicuous in the Caroline artistic and political milieu. The ultimate triumph in both *The City Wit* and *The Court Begger* of virtue over illicit opportunity gained by favoritism of birth or rank is part of that strong morality underlying all of the Bromean canon reaching out beyond the immediate concerns of his age.

CHAPTER 4

Gatherings of "Naughty-packs"

*T*HE *Weeding of Covent-Garden* (1632), *The Sparagus*
Garden (1635), *The New Academy* (1625-35), and *A Mad*
Couple Well Match't (1637-39) are all comedies of manners;
social satires exposing particular humors or the strivings of
various characters for falsely affected pseudograces. In these
plays the London citizen does not come off nearly so well. In
almost every instance he is either the gull or the guller who
becomes the main target of the ridicule for his foolishness and his
aspirations. He is rendered laughable, however, and not socially
castigated as he might be in a Jonsonian satire.

In addition, these plays utilize topographical references;
particular locations, immediately identifiable to the audience,
provide a meeting ground to which the characters, for whatever
reason, are drawn. Brome was not alone in using realistic London
references to catch the eye and laughter of the audience; both
James Shirley *(Hyde Park)* and Thomas Nabbes *(Covent Garden)*
produced plays the same year as *The Covent-Garden Weeded*
(1632) appeared.[1] Nor was the idea original; *Bartholomew Fair*,
although not a comedy of manners, had been an unqualified
success as early as 1614 and was published in 1631 just a year
before the vogue for place-realism caught on in the London
theater.[2]

I The Weeding of Covent-Garden

Brome acknowledged his debt to Jonson's play in the opening
sequence of *The Covent-Garden Weeded,* in which the central
structure of the play becomes clear. Cockbrain, a Justice of the
Peace, and Rooksbill, a "great Builder in *Covent Garden,*" are
admiring the architecture surrounding the new piazza. If only,
they agree, the tenants to the new houses were as worthy as the

structure. Unfortunately, like weeds, undesirable people spring up first in a new area. Cockbrain determines that he shall go about "unspied" and weed out these "enormities." "And so," he concludes, "as my Reverend Ancestor *Justice Adam Overdo*, was wont to say, In *Heaven's name and the King's*, and so for the good of the Commonwealth I will go about it" (B 1ᵛ; I,i). Thus a frame is established, similar to that of *Bartholomew Fair*, within which the episodes bringing about the "weeding" will take place and identification is made between Cockbrain and Jonson's well-meaning justice.

As in *Bartholomew Fair*, the framework is merely a device of location. The title of Brome's play and its subtitle, *The Middlesex Justice of the Peace*, are misleading and suggest that his original dramatic plan may have got out of hand. After citing the descriptive detail of the new garden, Theodore Miles concludes that "apart from the names of the rooms, such as 'Phoenix,' 'Dolphin,' 'Maidenhead,' and possibly the personality of the proprietor, the photograph is not very sharp. Throughout, Brome is concerned mainly with forwarding his very typical and conventional comedy of dupes and dupers."[3] Professor Floyd has pointed out that, although "in the looseness of its structure it is reminiscent of *Bartholomew Fair*, [*Covent-Garden Weeded*] is more closely related to *The Silent Woman*, since practically all of the action of the main plot has its origin in the exaggerated humor of one of the characters."[4] The character Will Crossewill is as fine an example of humor or proclivity as ever came from Jonson's pen. As his name indicates, he consistently acts contrary to any suggestion, and his children have learned to request or provoke the opposite of what they really desire. The playwright is attempting two rather loosely knit dramatic impulses working at the same time: the purging of the garden itself and the bringing together of various conflicting elements which move at the whim of Crossewill or countermove at the direction of those who would thwart him.

Crossewill is the visual representation of the polarities in attitudes and affectations of both plots. His eldest son, Gabriel, an excellent satire against the Puritans, affects a ridiculous religiosity[5] to "cross" his father for sending him away from Damaris, the women he loved. The younger son, Mihil, pretends to be so interested in the pious study of law that his father insists he leave his books lest he become as dull as Gabriel. Katherine,

Crossewill's daughter, says she wants a husband so her father will *not* get her one, and Damaris appears to be a *"Curtezan of Venice"* when actually she is a virtuous maid who is ultimately honestly married.

While these and other false poses are pursued, Cockbrain attempts to cleanse the garden of the riff-raff it has collected. His appearances are at best intermittent, and only with somewhat clumsy ineffectiveness does the playwright recall to the audience's mind the "weeding" theme designated in the title. At the beginning of Act V, Crossewill appears on stage alone, commenting upon a letter he has received from Cockbrain:

What has this Coxcomb *Cockbrain* writ me here? . . . A project he says here for the good of the Republic, Repudding. This fellow has instead of brains, a Cobweb in his Noddle. . . .He is ambitious to be called into authority by notice taken of some special service he is able to do the State aforehand. But what great service is he able to do it, or which way to undertake it, falls not in the reach of my imagination.

(F 7^r; V,i)

Although, as his name indicates, he does have "a Cobweb in his Noddle," Cockbrain's undertakings are far too vague to fall within the reach of the audience's imagination either.

To understand and appreciate Brome's artful characterization of Rooksbill, the "Builder" in Covent Garden, we must remember that parts of the famous London landmark were laid out by Inigo Jones, who is the target for Bromean satire elsewhere.[6] Brome is very subtle but the initial dialogue suggests that Rooksbill was intended to draw laughter at the expense of Inigo Jones,[7] the architect for the Russell estate. In his great admiration for the garden, the first thing Cockbrain singles out is "yond magnificent Piece, the Piazzo," one of the parts of the garden built first by Jones and opened in 1631. It "will excell that at *Venice,* by hearsay," Cockbrain goes on, although "(I ne'er travell'd)" (B1^r; I, i). Such association of Jones with Italy brings to mind Jonson's Introduction to *Hymenaei,* in which he attacks the brainless who would ignore the "full tables" of his poetic feast and take instead *"Italian* herbs, picked [by Inigo Jones], and made into a salad" of stage designs.[8]

Still referring to the architectural wonders of Venice, Cockbrain continues, "A hearty blessing on their brains, honors, and wealths, that are Projectors, Furtherers, and Performers of

such great works." That Rooksbill[9] is presented as one of the
"Projectors, Furtherers, and Performers," one who copies or acts
upon the creations of others, confirms the characterization of
Inigo Jones in *The Court Begger*. To Brome and the other
professional dramatists of Stuart England, Jones was a parasite
who lived off or, in this case, built upon the artistic talents of
others, interested only in wealth, social position, and royal favor,
and not in creative originality. After crediting Italian genius,
Cockbrain ignores Rooksbill's talents and comments only on the
money he has gained from "such Structures," then praises the
Surveyor ("what e'er he was") responsible for wedding "strength
to beauty; state to uniformity, commodiousness to perspicuity."
All Rooksbill concerns himself with is the worth of the tenants
who pay his rents. He is quickly assured not to worry; the "lime"
and "hair" that are the builders' foundations are as "soil to dung"
(B 1^v; I, i) to the land. With that final satiric thrust toward Jones,
Brome turns his attention to the Justice's project for weeding.[10] A
further identification of Jones as Rooksbill occurs near the end of
Act I, when Nicolas is asked whether the "great Builder" is his
father. He replies affirmatively and adds that he hopes Rooksbill
"will be the first shall lay his bones i' the new Church, though
the Church-yard be too good for him before 'tis consecrated"
(B 8^{r-v}; I,i), an allusion to Jones's construction of St. Paul's
Church, which began in 1631. In addition, considering that Jones
was a known Roman Catholic, the audience would be amused by
Rooksbill's exaggerated admiration for Gabriel's extreme
puritanism. Such use of topographical locations and interests
associated with the architect gives a sharper satiric thrust to the
place-realism in *The Covent-Garden Weeded* than has previously been realized.

In general, *The Weeding of Covent-Garden* has a rough,
boisterous good humor about it. In addition to the creation of
Crossewill and Rooksbill, Brome again shows his skill in the
characterization of bawdy characters within a loose low-level
plot. Mun Clotpoll is a gull who wishes nothing more than to be a
part of the "fraternity" of "both Philoblathicus and Philobat-
ticus" and is quickly taken by Captain Driblow. His name, which
means blockhead, identifies him for the audience and he
bumbles his way thick-headedly from the stage at the end of the
play as unenlightened as when he came on it. The bawd, the
"Countess of Codpiece-Row," and her punks have the ribald

good humor that Brome achieves in most of his low comic figures.

Quite rightly, R. J. Kaufmann has chosen to concentrate his critical attention upon the social and moral issues inherent within extreme paternalism which has led to polarization of filial reaction.[11] In *The Covent-Garden Weeded,* the whole concept of irrational and unnatural parental authority is reduced to absurdity. There is no more compromise between Gabriel's Puritan "brethren" and Mihil's "Brothers of the Blade and Baton"than there is room for the "Sisters of the Scabbard" (open prostitution) in Covent Garden. They are, rather, analyzed and ridiculed as the kind of excess which emerges from extreme authority. Clumsy reconciliation is achieved in the final lines of the play when separated lovers and divided families are rejoined, but at base the play relies rather weakly on satiric exposure and warning rather than on moral reconciliation.

II   The Sparagus Garden

> I had more to say—
> The Title, too, may prejudice the Play.
> It says the *Sparagus Garden;* if you look
> To feast on that, the Title spoils the Book.
> We have yet a taste of it, which he doth lay
> I'th midst of the journey, like a Bait by the way:
> Now see with Candor: As our *Poet's* free,
> Pray let be so your *Ingenuity.*
>
> (A 4 ʳ)

In these comments from the Prologue to *The Sparagus Garden,* Brome seems to be aware that he is following a fad in his use of topical references and that too close identification of the audience with the setting of a play can distract attention from its thematic matter. Perhaps the "detached" use of local color discussed by Theodore Miles is the playwright's attempt to cope with the problem. All the material having to do with the garden, Miles points out, appears in the eleven scenes which make up Act III; only five "contribute to the action," while the remaining are simple " 'shots' of various aspects of the Sparagus Garden" grafted upon the play and therefore tending to halt the dramatic movement.[12]

In spite of the minor structural flaws and occasional distractions, the comic method by which Brome centers upon the thematic interests and exposes false values is ingenious. In each of the intrigues which complicate the play, irrational and unnatural behavior is ridiculed through the same comic device: at each level of the play—pseudoromantic, satiric, and farcical— a familiar situation or a common metaphor usually taken seriously or figuratively is rendered comically concrete.

The pseudoromantic plot is a comic adaptation of *Romeo and Juliet,* in which the Italian Montagues and Capulets become English Touchwoods and Strikers. Brome's young lovers, Samuel and Annabel, are laughable in their extravagant declarations of undying devotion. Rather than taking desperate tragic measures to overcome parental opposition, they engage in ingenious trickery which gives rise to much of the bawdy dialogue. The frustrating plot complications which have made their families enemies are unraveled only when Annabel's swollen belly proves to be nothing more than a cushion. As for those who would thwart the natural celebrations of love, each of the parental *pharmakos* figures is more concerned with outwitting the other than with the happiness of his offspring. Their animosity is an "ancient grudge" for which the young lovers must suffer until they outwit their parents. Friswood, the parallel to Juliet's nurse, is as garrulous as her counterpart but is more actively engaged in the plot developments; eventually she marries the heroine's grandfather, whose bed she has shared for years.

Auxiliary to the romantic mockery is a satire on the making of a gentleman. Tim Hoyden, a ninny from Somersetshire, is convinced he can be purged of the yeoman side of his lineage and become "a finicall City wit, and a superfinicall Court wit too" (D 2ᵛ; II,iii). The purging, however, is not figurative but actual. R. J. Kaufmann calls this "literalizing in action" the concept of base and highborn blood.[13] The poor gull actually allows his "foul rank blood of Bacon and Pease-porrige" to be drained off and replaced with what his parasites assure him is gentleman's blood. His diet is also designed to purge the "malignant baseness" of his present state so that ultimately his blood will be "as high as any Gentleman's lineally descended from the loins of King Cadwalder" (D 3ᵛ; II,iii). Such a gull was familiar to the London audience, as was Tim Hoyden's brother Tom. Much more practical in nature (though not above indulging in the odd scheme for his own betterment), Tom Hoyden supplies the visual representation of country unaffectedness, complete with Somerset dialect. These two, the social aspirant and the solid rustic, are among the progenitors of Congreve's Witwoud and Sir Wilful Witwoud some sixty years later.

One of the gullers who preys on Tim Hoyden has troubles of his own. Poor Brittleware has a problem wife, Rebecca, who wants so desperately to become pregnant that her husband fears she will turn to some other bedfellow. Here Brome converts another stock comic situation to farce. Rebecca's determination to indulge in all the strange yearnings thought to be brought on by pregnancy (even if the actual state is so far denied her) allows the playwright to engage in nonsense based upon "literalizing" a common phenomenon. He can also indulge in further bawdy innuendo in which "man-litter," *"Paul's Steeple,"* and the "knight of the burning Pestle" all take on sexual overtones. Even asparagus becomes a phallic symbol. Rebecca is encouraged to go to the "Garden of delight" where, Money-lacks assures her,

. . . you may have it [asparagus] dressed and eaten in the due kind; and there it is so provocative, and so quick in the hot operation, that none dare eat it, but those that carry their coolers with 'em, presently to delay, or take off the delightful fury it fills 'em with.

(D 1^r; II,ii)

The Sparagus Garden itself merely provides a locality to which all of the characters come at one time or another. A kind of high-class brothel where immorality is encouraged, the garden provides a microcosm for the kind of self-indulgences engaged in by the London middle-class citizenry, whether it be cheating in money or sex, or gulling for economic or physical satisfaction. *The Sparagus Garden* is, in other words, a Bromean *Bartholomew Fair,* without the "place" providing the dramatic unity which Jonson's fair did. As Clarence E. Andrews says, "The whole effect of witnessing the play must have been much like trying to watch a five-ring circus with side-shows added."[14] The author too was obviously not happy with the play and apologizes for its weaknesses in the epilogue:

At first we made not boast, and still we fear,
We have not answer'd expectation here,
Yet give us leave to hope, as hope to live,

That you will grace, as well as Justice give.

(L 4ᵛ)

III   The New Academy

The dating of *The New Academy, or The New Exchange* is difficult. There are some indications it may have been written as early as 1626 when Brome was still under Jonson's tutelage and produced, as Bentley suggests, as a "rival attraction to James Shirley's *The School of Compliment* (1625).[15] Both plays include a kind of mock academy where social aspirants attempt to learn affected graces, both involve a lost child (a daughter, Felice, in *The School of Compliment* and a son, Papillion, in *The New Academy)*, and both effect their resolutions with the rediscovery of lost children and the sorting out of brothers and sisters. In each play there is an episode in which a supposedly doting wife turns out to be a shrew. However, both *The School of Compliment* and Jonson's *Bartholomew Fair* (the progenitor of place-realism drama) were printed for the first time in 1631, and a plethora of such plays, including *The New Academy*, more than likely followed these publications.

Besides noting the actual existence of a New Exchange, a gathering place in the Strand which became popular in the early 1630s, R. J. Kaufmann draws an association between *The New Academy* and the popular French acting group whose performances took place in a riding academy in Drury Lane in 1635. On this basis he dates *The New Academy* in 1635 and suggests that it was the first play written by Brome under his first Salisbury Court contract.[16] Subsequent evidence shows that Kaufmann is probably right. Brome's reply to the suit brought against him by the Salisbury Court company states that *Sparagus Garden* was produced at Salisbury Court, but before he signed the first contract; he says then he wrote two more after the contract but before plague closed the theaters. *The Queen and Concubine* accounts for one of these and, unless there is an unknown play of which there is no record, *The New Academy* is the other.

The title indicates the theme of the play and the action, although turning upon French affectations, includes as much satire against those English who would adopt French manners as against the kind of posturing they admire. The well-spring of the satire, however, is much deeper than mere mockery of French intruders, for the play's mating intrigues deal with various aspects of the reconstructed and degenerated neo-Platonic love conventions which had been reintroduced into the London court by Queen Henrietta Maria. Professor Upham explains that "Platonism as an active working principle was not accepted by the English courtiers of the time in its really serious and austere aspect. . . . It was Platonism given a gallant or courtly twist; welcomed. . .as an excuse for zealous love-making"[17] and it had filtered down to become the vogue for those who would affect to be what they are not. Among the Platonics were Davenant and Suckling,[18] so it is not surprising that Richard Brome falls into the category of the anti-Platonics, whose "prevailing tone" was one of "satirico-comic deprecation" of the new fashion.[19] The pretensions, the pseudographs of his characters form a thin veneer of politeness which fails to conceal irrationality, licentiousness, or self-indulgence.

Although not as skillfully interrelated as in more successful Brome plays, the familiar multiple plotting of *The New Academy* allows its author to strike out at current fashions and at particular human follies. If there is a central character to this play it is Old Matchil, if only by virtue of the fact that his crisis in the opening scenes and the decisions which arise from it set the romantic and satiric actions in motion. Matchil and his closest friend, a French gentleman named Lafoy, had exchanged children a number of years ago. Young Matchil had been reared in France and Gabriella Lafoy in England. Now, however, Matchil receives news that his son is dead, and he responds in a series of excessive reactions. First, he tells us, he sank into sorrow, but then he set aside "puling grief" and determined to revenge himself on Lafoy, whom he blamed for his loss. In a rage he not only dismisses Gabriella from his house but also his own daughter when she pleads loyalty to Gabriella. Because of the exchange of children, the son and daughter of Matchil do not know each other, and neither do those of Lafoy. When all four of the young people arrive together at the New Academy, the lack of sibling awareness leads to each brother becoming sworn to his own sister. In the closing scenes of the play, however, the new exchange of partners and vows takes place. The love interest of itself carries little of the mockery of affected manners which characterizes the other levels of the play. When they meet at the New Academy, however, the unscrupulous Stripgood passes the

young ladies off as women of easy virtue and the young men as
tutors lately arrived from France. They become Brome's means
to expose the various gulls who frequent the academy either for
sexual self-indulgence, licentious patter, or for what they fancy is
social refinement.

Meanwhile Matchil, with all the drama of "a plague on both
your houses," determines to remarry. When his associates remind
him that he has been "King of mirth" since becoming a widower,
he brags,

> . . . I will marry [a woman]
> That I foreknow can never disobey me
> And I'll defy the devil to dishonest her.
>
> (I 1^v; I,i)

This he does; he weds his "drudge" and the new situation gives
rise to still another Platonic mockery at the satiric level of the
play. Rachael turns into a wife who is more than Matchil can
handle. Much to his delight she is at first quick to defend herself
and her marriage against the snobbish jibes of Lady Nestlecock,
but Matchil's delight changes to chagrin when she attacks him
for being an officious busybody. The marriage is seriously
threatened when Rachael's determination to be a lady leads her
to grant the wily Valentine the mock-courtly position of *midon*
or "servant [as] Gentlewomen use it" (K 8^r; II,i). By offsetting
the battle of the sexes seen in courtly wooing and disjoining
natural man-wife relations, Brome attacks another convention—
the false notions of obedience and the lack of mutual respect in
marriage. Together these constitute a condemnation of marriage
for convenience or practicality rather than for more natural
reasons. Matchil finally recognizes that the "moving cause" of all
his troubles has been his "own impetuous rashness." Realizing
that Rachael's behavior is "but to try mastery," a "disease," he
says, which is "general among all women," he makes a deal with
her. As the knight to the "loathly lady" in Chaucer's "The Wife
of Bath's Tale," Matchil yields himself to her "thraldom." If she
will preserve his honor publicly, he will admit her command
privately. The arrangement, quaintly Elizabethan rather than
Caroline, promises to be as mutually respectful as that Avergus
made to Dorigen in "The Franklin's Tale" and leads to the same
promise of compatibility.

Coupled with the marital complications of Matchil and his wife are those of Rafe Camelion and his aspiring wife, Hannah. Professor Sedge has already called attention to the main comic method of the Rafe-Hannah plot, which is the transposition of the neo-Platonic creed.

Camelion's "humour" [he says] is an excessive desire to prove he is not jealous of his wife's behaviour. . . . The point of Brome's presentation of Camelion's excessive anxiety not to seem jealous is to satirize the state of society in which the natural relationship of trust between man and wife has been undermined by the introduction of a new ethic that attempts to put trust between man and wife on the level of external etiquette.[20]

Rafe, however, is a knight whose errant jaunts abroad are highjinks at the ducking pond down the street; Hannah's *midon* is the same Valentine who was quick to offer his services to Rachael Matchil. Valentine swears Hannah is his "Faery" and he is bound to her by the courtly vow of secrecy, but he is a cynical rogue whose every action belies his exaggerated declarations of service. Such undercutting reduces the degenerated pretensions of Platonic love to absolute absurdity.

At the farcical level, another kind of knight is mocked in the person of Sir Swithin Whilmby, "the crying knight," who woos Lady Nestlecock in outrageous poetry. His daughter, Mrs. Blitheshort, has the most significant Bromean comment on the whole nonsense of the low comic level of the play. After listening to the mad cross-wooings for a while, she pleads,

> Love, as I shall adore thee for a deity,
> Rid me of this ridiculous society.
>
> (K 7^r; II,i)

It is only after all the various intrigues and relationships are set in motion in the first two acts that the "new academy" or "Acomedy," as Nestlecock's witless son calls it, is introduced. From then on, the academy and what it represents provide both the unity of place and opportunity for satire as all the characters visit this so-called school of manners and compliment. Joyce and Gabriella, taken there by their uncle, act as bait to draw in lecherous youths. When they question the effects of their behavior on their public reputation, Stripgood claims their actions are vindicated because they bring "Justice" upon folly. This draws a sharp retort designed to attack false notions of courtship rituals, for the "courtly Gypsy tricks" taught to women, the ladies quickly point out, "trench upon" their modesties. The meeting of the girls with their own brothers and the sincerity in their ultimate cross-matching serve to emphasize the ludicrous poses affected by the others.

One by one, the masks of pseudomanners are discarded willingly or by force of situation. For all her airs of propriety, Lady Nestlecock slips into common language when angered. "I'll put her by her school tricks," she shouts when her son is called a "walking dunghill," and "not only unmask, but unskin her face too, and she come over my heir apparent with such *Billingsgate* Compliments" (N 1ʳ; IV,i). One by one, the mock knights are ridiculed into reality. Sir Swithin Whilmby recognizes his niece's right to choose her own husband and gives over his tears.

> I will no longer whine.
> Heaven give you joy [he says to Blithe], As you
>   are you're own, y'are mine.
>
> (O 5ᵛ; V,i)

When Rafe thinks he is losing money, he gives way to jealousy and then is brought sharply to his senses with the realization of his previous folly. Valentine is exposed as a "boasting libertine," and Matchil admits to his own "wilfulness" and "officiousness" when true love finds a way.

The ending with its reconciliations is the most contrived of any of Brome's plays. The revelation of previously unknown relationships and the introduction of a *deus ex machina* are piecemeal devices used to unravel cross-intrigues. In addition, extraneous stage entertainment intrudes too often upon the action. It is true that the extravagant French dances, part of the instruction provided by the academy, are affectations of foreign and unnatural pseudograces, but both these and the intrusive songs violate the unity of action and divert the audience's attention from the thematic anti-Platonism. Swinburne, however, was too harsh when he called it a "tangled and huddled comedy. . . worth reading once as a study of manners and language."[21] Like *The Sparagus Garden, The New Academy* does have merit as an example of a rather sophisticated comic method; but unfortunately both plays tend to disintegrate into diversion.

IV   A Mad Couple Well Match't

Unlike *The Weeding of Covent-Garden, The Sparagus Garden,* and *The New Academy,* the title *A Mad Couple Well Match't* does not immediately indicate a specific location. Its place-realism is quickly established, however, so that there is no doubt the players inhabit an area of London known intimately to the theater audience. Moments into the opening scene, the servant, Wat, tries to encourage Careless, the wild hero of the main plot, to think of some new project to improve their desperate financial straits. Careless moans,

> I cannot, nor will I trouble my brains to think of any, I will rather die here in *Ram Alley,* or walk down to the *Temple,* and lay myself down alive, in the old Synagogue, cross-legged among the Monumental Knights there, till I turn marble with 'em.
>
> (B1^v-2^r; I, i)

Later, when Careless has been taken in by the Thrivewells, he says,

> I need no more ensconcing now in *Ram Alley,* nor the Sanctuary of *Whitefriars,* the Forts of *Fullers-rents,* and *Milford-lane,* whose walls are daily battered with the curses of bawling creditors.
>
> (C 8^r; II,i)

The whole area indicated in these speeches was one of evil reputation, inhabited by bawds, debtors, and the like. Ram Alley,[22] with all the sexual connotations of goatish lechery, is where Careless has enjoyed his whore (and where Wat, incidentally, has also enjoyed her), and it is where he returns from his uncle's house for his excesses of "Wine, Roaring, Whoring" (D8^v; III,i).

The area of Ram Alley is also where Alicia Saleware, the mercer's wife, has cuckolded her husband with Sir Valentine Thrivewell and any other man she can bed. The fact that she is called "Ally" only makes the sexual punning on Ram Alley more descriptive of her favorite pastime. Contrasted to Ram Alley is the home of Thrivewell and Lady Thrivewell; there the sexual act is actually only consummated once when Phoebe, the whore, enters Careless's bed in place of Lady Thrivewell in a well-arranged bed-trick.

Brome has left the reference in the play's title ambiguous. Both the Thrivewells and the Salewares are coupled in mad arrangements, and in each case the arrangement is designed to expose the flaws of the aristocratic fetish for Platonic non-jealousy, a favorite target for Bromean satire. This courtly game is handled quite differently from the one in *The New Academy*, even though there are certain similarities in structure and character.[23] In *A Mad Couple* the multiplicity of mating dances suggests that the title may also refer to the variety of mad couplings in which all are well matched in their intrigues and connivings.

The first of these arrangements, that of the Thrivewells, is quite remarkable in its urbanity and in its clear revelation of the changing status of women in marriage. In answer to his wife's queries on his obvious discomfiture and indisposition, Thrivewell confesses to an adulterous liaison with Alicia Saleware. In addition to priming her all year by shopping in her husband's store, he has paid Ally a hundred pounds for one sexual encounter, thinking after "to deal Rent-free." Now the merchant's wife demands each "new purchase [be] at the same former rate, and so for all times after" (C 1r; I,i). Lady Thrivewell appears to register shock only at such unreasonable prices and to accept that confession absolves him of the crime, but in reality she determines to teach him a lesson. Only after making him believe that she too has committed adultery does he come to realize that confession does *not* mitigate injury, that what is sauce for the gander *can* be sauce for the goose, and that friendship and trust are as much a part of marriage as are practicability and heir-getting.

With Alicia Saleware and her husband, friendship and trust are carried to an absurd extreme. Saleware is a good fellow but stupid enough to abide by a "Covenant" that says he and his wife will model their conduct after those of the court. Thus, he must not hang over her all the time, or even share a room with her—"that were most uncourtly."[24] Neither must he question where she goes or what she does—that were untrusting. She reminds him when he asks what "Honor" Lord Lovely, "a wencher," has lately done for them,

Did you not Covenant with me that I should wear what I pleased, and
what my Lord liked, that I should be as Lady-like as I would, or as my
Lord desired; that I should come, and go at mine own pleasure, or as my
Lord required; and that we should be always friends and call so, not
after the silly manner of Citizen and Wife, but in the high courtly way?

(E 5ᵛ; III,i)

Brome's main satiric thrust is clearly against the aristocratic
code and those who would pretend to it. Saleware's stupidity at
accepting such an artificial relationship is linked first to the
mercer's own pretentions to courtly behavior and then to his
uxoriousness and, finally, to his avarice. Informed that his wife
will not share a bedroom with him in her new house, Saleware
fantasizes, "But I shall have a chamber in your house and next to
yours. Then in my Gown and Slippers Friend at Midnight—or at
the first Cock—." But no, he must make a choice.

Soft for stumbling Friend [his wife answers], I'll do you any honourable
offices with my Lord, as by obtaining suits for you, for which you must
look out, and find what you may fitly beg out of his power, and by
courtly favour. But keep your Shop still Friend, and my Lord will bring
and send you such customs, that your Neighbours shall envy your
wealth, and not your Wife; you shall have such comings in abroad and at
home, that you shall be the first head nominated in the next Sheriff
season, but I with my Lord will keep you from pricking. Be you a
Citizen still Friend, 'tis enough I am Courtly.

(E 6ᵛ; III,i)

Thus Saleware's agreement to do "as the sweet Lord will have
it," couched in a blasphemous paraphrase of "God's will be
done," becomes part of the viciousness of the whole circle of
citizen affectation and greed.

In the main plot Alicia Saleware is matched by Careless,
nephew to the Thrivewells. He, too, couples lechery with lucre;
his machinations are also totally self-indulgent and immoral.
Thomas Saleware is linked with Sir Valentine Thrivewell. Both
are guilty of their own folly and are easy dupes to the plots of
wife and nephew. The only admirable character is Lady
Thrivewell, and even she is forced to deal with immorality on its
own terms and at its own level in order to outwit both Alicia and
Careless. Whether Alicia and Careless ever actually learn a
lesson and show any signs of reform is another matter. Professor
Sedge suggests,

Brome's play clearly exposes the dangerous excess in feminism that can result from the Platonic non-jealousy ethic. Alicia is humbled when her intention to cuckold her husband [still another time] is foiled by his arrival at the crucial moment. By her wits Alicia tries to save face but she has been frightened into a realization of the error of her behaviour and her submissive reply to her husband's demand for a return to a more natural relationship between man and wife suggest that she has learned from her error.[25]

The folly of the doctrine that "friendship itself allows all liberty" is exposed when Alicia is caught in her own trap, but whether she is truly repentant is another question, for she has shown remarkable ability to tack to whatever wind is blowing. At the end of the play Lord Lovely has cast her off with some pious words of advice, but Saleware thinks she has just been trying to make him jealous all the time. What other choice has she but to be "loving man and wife henceforward" (H 1ʳ; V,ii)? As for Careless, there is no sign of regret for past action or declaration of future virtuous intent whatsoever. Nevertheless he does end up with a "humorous" wife who is attracted to him and determines to marry him for the very licentiousness which makes him a scoundrel. Perhaps some virtue can be found in his willingness to marry his whore and make her honest, but his reasons for action never change. He trained Phoebe in sex and therefore she can hold him "Tick tack"; she "knows her play" and thus will please his bed (G 6ᵛ; V,ii), but as soon as a better opportunity arises with Crostwill, the wealthy widow, he switches to her. No word of affection or respect passes; rather, he promises lustily,

> —at night, at night, at night—
> We'll get the Boy that shall become a Knight.
>
> (H 1ᵛ; V,ii)

The critics have assailed *A Mad Couple* on moral grounds more than any other Brome play. Schelling, one of the most vociferous in this century, says, *A Mad Couple well Matched* . . .reaches depths of coarseness and vulgarity. . . . The complaisance and unaffectedness of the immorality . . . lie far lower than the worst of Middleton, and with some other passages of Brome relieve Dryden and Wycherley of the odium of having debased English drama below depths previously reached in the reign of the virtuous King Charles."[26] Forty years later, Floyd persists in this vein: "One of the coarsest and most revolting plays presented before the Restoration, [*A Mad Couple*] deals with the shameless conduct of 'a young wilde heir' whose very lecherousness wins him the wealthy 'humorous' young widow for a wife."[27] Even Kaufmann, though he admits it to be a "successful achievement" and a "skillful city comedy," links *A Mad Couple* with the Restoration and dismisses it as "the most obscene" of Brome's works, "worth reading," but requiring "little critical comment."[28]

Offsetting these pejorative assessments is a group of less one-sided critics. Swinburne takes a much more objective view. "*A Mad Couple Well Matched,*" he says, "is very clever, very coarse, and rather worse than dubious in the bias of its morality; but there is no fault to be found with the writing or the movement of the play; both style and action are vivid and effective throughout." "Variety of satirical observation," he goes on, "and fertility of comic invention, with such strong sound English as might be expected from a disciple of his master's, give to this as to others of Brome's comedies a quality which may fairly and without flattery be called Jonsonian."[29] Charles E. Guardia adds to this praise for integrated and unified structure. "Every thread," he says, "is so completely involved in the others that to take one would necessitate a considerable change in the rest."[30] There is no doubt that *A Mad Couple* is one of the best structured of Brome's city comedies. The three main threads of narrative are introduced in the first three scenes and are kept integrated to the final resolution, and the characterizations are consistent. Although one sex disguise is necessary for the intrigues, the play has none of the artificial devices that weaken others of the comedies, and it is remarkably free of extra-dramatic entertainment.

It is against the "matter" of the play that most adverse comment has been directed. In dealing with the argument as to whether poetic justice is violated, Elizabeth Cook explains, "There is really a confusion of two standards in his [Brome's] time," that of an earlier age which rewarded virtue and punished vice, a standard badly abused by Caroline writers who could and did include the grossest of scenes only to justify them in the last act as trials of virtue; and the Jonsonian satire "which claimed to purge vice by making it ridiculous: a theory that could be used to justify the grossest exhibition as the most moral."[31] To Brome's credit, he does not resort to a miraculous conversion of Careless and Alicia at the end of the play. If they seem unpunished, we might remember that Subtle, Face, and Dol Common, worthy of "the longest cut at night," also escaped unscathed in Jonson's *Alchemist.* All three will live to gull another day.

Everyone is neatly paired off at the end of *A Mad Couple Well Match't;* marriages which have become shaky through mutual folly are, at least for the time being, still solvent, and new unions are made. But Lady Thrivewell warns the widow Crostwill that she is "undone," and this may suggest that marriage based on Careless's sexual terms will be as weak as one on any other single base. Furthermore, Wat's willingness to take the whore *and* the hundred pounds Crostwill offers, suggests another Saleware marriage in the making. Wat's words to Careless,

This woman has been mine as much as yours, she has done as much with me for Offices, and Service I have done for her, as she has done with you for Love and Money. . .

(G 7ʳ; V,ii)

certainly suggest that Phoebe will be another Alicia. The conclusion is very much within the Jonsonian tradition: vice is exposed, and the implication of a moral norm only implied by inversion. If mortals persist (as they almost invariably do) in establishing false codes and standards for natural human relationships, they will continue to be fools.

CHAPTER 5

The Tragicomedies: "Fresh Flora after the Blasts of Winter"

I N the Prologue to *A Jovial Crew*, the speaker laments what he sees as "these sad and tragic days" when "Jovial mirth is now grown out of fashion." With a straight face, he denies the promise of merriment that his title might imply. Rather, says Prologue:

> (*Our Comic Writer finding that* Romances
> *Of Lovers, through much travel and distress,*
> *'Till it be thought, no Power can redress*
> *The afflicted Wanderers, though stout Chivalry*
> *Lend all his aid for their delivery;*
> *'Till, lastly, some impossibility*
> *Concludes all strife, and makes a Comedy)*
> *Finding (he says) such stories bear the sway,*
> *Near as he could, he has composed a Play.*

(a 2ᵛ)

The irony is that *A Jovial Crew* is not a tragicomedy. In fact, the words of the Prologue allow the playwright to mock the prevailing tragicomic fashion which had been popular since the early part of the century and which he parodies so successfully in *The Love-sick Court*.[1] Surprisingly, considering his later mockery of the form, Brome had himself in the earlier part of his career written two tragicomedies: *The Queen's Exchange* (1631–32) and *The Queen and Concubine* (1635–36). *The Queen's Exchange*, however, was written immediately after Brome began a dramatic career independent of Jonson and it may be that, although his former mentor would not have approved, the young playwright was eager to try his hand at the genre which was so popular in the acting houses.

Also Brome was quick to take advantage of theatrical fad.[2] In addition to his own *The Northern Lass,* in which Constance's senses are turned to confusion by love (and the lost *Love-sick Maid* which we might assume dealt in some way with love's maladies), Jonson's *The New Inn* and a spate of plays by John Ford,[3] which probed the psychology of distempered love appeared in the London theaters between 1627 and 1633. Although love melancholy generally interested dramatists throughout the Renaissance, the particular popularity of dramatizing the psychology of distraction during these years may have led Brome to pursue it in *The Queen's Exchange.* Indeed, the possibility in Robert Greene's *Penelope's Web* to explore the matter even further may have led to *The Queen and Concubine* when Brome was looking for a subject with public appeal in 1635–36, after he signed to write for Salisbury Court.

I   The Queen's Exchange

Taking as its setting some obscure Anglo-Saxon time, *The Queen's Exchange* is basically imaginary history worked into episodic adventures which have a strong flavor of medieval romance. The tone of the opening scenes is somewhat serious and tense, in the manner of the Fletcherian mode of tragicomedy. Very quickly a sense of the juxtaposition of opposites is established between sincerity and affectation in the romantic and in the quasi-tragic plots. Bertha, Queen of the Saxons, flattered by the proxy wooing of an ambassador from the King of Northumbria, expresses her desire to wed the foreign monarch. All her lords acquiesce to her wishes save one, Segebert, who warns her against the match. Calling the other lords "sycophants," Segebert reminds the Queen of her responsibility to the needs of the nation and of her father's wish that she should choose a husband from among the nobles of her own dominion rather than subject her nation to the "thraldom" of a foreign prince. For his pains and his indecorous "If you knew anything," Segebert is banished from the kingdom for daring to oppose his "prince's purposes" in the same way Kent is banished in *King Lear.*

The other scene of Act I introduces the second plot, which resembles *Lear* even more. Segebert, before taking leave, bids farewell to his three children. From each, he asks an expression of their gratitude. Mildred, his daughter, weeps and would plead with the Queen for her father. This Segebert forbids; he orders her to stay away from the court and particularly from the Northumbrian ambassador, who has been wooing for himself and has succeeded in obtaining Mildred's picture. Offa, the younger of the two sons, declares his indebtedness in such excessive terms that Segebert leaves him in charge of the family estates. Anthynus, the elder son, reminds Segebert with what scorn his father had viewed the excessive flattery of the court. He only asks that he be allowed to follow his father into exile.

Brome's reliance upon *King Lear* is obvious. The willfulness of the Queen, her susceptibility to flattery, and the banishment of Segebert all shadow Lear's actions. Segebert is at once Kent in his frankness and honesty and Gloucester in his having one loyal and one conniving son. Anthynus is characteristic of Edgar in his devotion to his father and of Cordelia in his refusal to declare unnatural love.[4] Offa, although not illegitimate, is as hypocritical and threatening as Edmund. The only features which intrude upon the prevailing seriousness of the action are the caricatures which the fawning lords present and the exaggeration to the point of ridiculousness of the effusion with which the Northumbrian king is described as adoring the Queen's picture. Yet the very quality of these excesses belies the anticipation that *The Queen's Exchange* will follow the awesome grandeur of Shakespeare's solemn tragedy. At least the romantic involvements foreshadow no disastrous outcome. The Queen's willfulness is folly, not deep-seated perversion; she is piqued by Segebert's refusal, not enraged.[5] Only the impending fortunes (or misfortunes) of Segebert and Anthynus are unrelieved by comic expectation. However, the suspension between tragic foreshadowing and comic resolution demanded by tragicomedy is only successful when the same characters are involved in actions which anticipate the possibility of either outcome. The first act of *The Queen's Exchange* sets in motion not one tragicomic plot but what appear to be two separate actions, one promising comedy and the other threatening tragedy. Even the devices used to link the two plots, Segebert's position as advisor to the Queen and Theodrick's devotion to Mildred, are never central issues again. Indeed, these four characters, important though they may be in providing dramatic impetus, slip into secondary roles. Only with the introduction of Osriik, the

Northumbrian king, does a clearer line of action take shape, loose and improbable though it may be, and a pattern of characterization emerge.

In the opening scene of Act II, Osriik of Northumbria makes plans for his forthcoming marriage to Queen Bertha. At first, he too seems excessive in his doting over the picture of his betrothed and in his response to Theodrick's praise of her beauty. When he sees the picture of Mildred, however, the Queen's likeness drops from his hand as he quickly shifts his adoration. He tries to cover his confused state but an aside,

> . . . What kind of Changeling am I?
> A wild confusion rumbles in my brain,
> My thoughts are all at strife,
>
> (C 2^r; II,i)

reveals his dilemma. He falls into a sick swoon and his physicians are called for. Although Osriik is later described as being sleepless, sighing, and seeking solitary groves, his condition is not merely that of the love-struck courtly lover. Osriik knows that he suffers not only from "raging passions" but also because he "slight[s] the queen" to whom he is betrothed and because he has unjustly punished Theodrick with banishment (D 3^v; III,i). His distraction comes not only from the heart but also, as Lawrence Babb explains, because "a fierce battle between love and right reason takes place in the mind of the King";[6] or, to use Jackson I. Cope's term, Osriik is suffering from "ruptured" reason.[7] Only when the circumstances of Anthynus's arrival in Northumbria permit him to travel incognito to West Saxony to woo and win Mildred does his mind become fully ordered again.

Osriik is not alone in experiencing "a Chaos of confused thoughts." Anthynus, having been separated from his father when they were set upon by the patricidal Offa, finds himself in a wood not far from the Northumbrian court. Just as he determines to appeal to Northumbria for aid, he hears music and a "strange benumbedness" comes over him. Transfixed, he views a prophetic pageant of six Saxon kings. Each approaches him, then they *"fall into a dance,"* and finally each leads his successor from the stage. The last *"takes up Anthynus, and leaves him standing upright"* (D 4^v; III,i). Anthynus thinks that the possibility of succession to the throne of Wessex is "more idle

than a dream can be," but the "whirlwind" in his mind
overcomes him and he faints.

Still another "secret instigation" guides Anthynus's destiny
after he is carried to court by Northumbrian hunters who
mistake him for Osriik. Thinking their king distempered by a
"languishing love" which can be cured by hastening his marriage,
the lords have sent for Bertha. Anthynus's impulse to "unfold this
mystery" is stilled by a *"Genius"* who whispers to him. Realizing
this "good Angel"[8] leads him to the fulfillment of the prophecy
of royal succession, he follows its "inspiration" and weds Queen
Bertha (F 1^{r-v}; IV,i). As these experiences are given no
psychological explanation, Professor Cope refers to Anthynus's
state as "raptured" reason.[9]

In Professor Cope's consideration of the play (and he is one of
the few critics to treat its better aspects seriously), the terms
used to describe Osriik's and Anthynus's mental states are
excellent, but he has left out the third member of Brome's triad
of characters, Offa, for Brome is exploring ruptured, raptured,
and rapine reason. Offa's derangement is not urged on by any
kind of love such as induced the other two to mental
enthrallment, but rather the lack of it. His evil "genius" leads
him first to plot against father and brother and, when he thinks
them dead, he celebrates in what is only a mock debate with his
conscience (E 2^v; IV,i). When incestuous lust is added to
ambition, the result is total depravity. Unlike Giovanni in Ford's
'Tis Pity She's a Whore[10] or Placilla in Brome's *The Love-sick
Court,* Offa's attempt to justify his desires is not reason doing
battle with passion, but his endeavor to persuade Mildred to his
lust. His mind is so diabolic that it is little wonder that later,
when the hired assassins whom he thought he had killed rise
from the ground as if ghosts from hell, Offa goes stark, raving
mad.

Brome's hierarchal pattern of characterization is clear: on the
heroic, almost celestial level, is high-minded Anthynus,
"Heaven's justice," "by an Angel spoke[n to]," "sanctimonious
virtue"; on the realistic level, the fallible Osriik is "brain-
crack'd," "full of frenetic humors," and the victim of "wavering
inconstancy"; at the infernal level, the murderous Offa,
"haunted by sprites," is a "Perfidious Patricide," an "Incestuous
monster." The conclusion of the play brings all three on stage
and Anthynus's words,

> 'Tis a day of grace,
> And we are taught by heaven's abundant mercy
> Shewn upon us by our expectation,
> To imitate that goodness,
>
> (G 2^r; V,i)

are directed as much to the theater audience as to the assembled court. For Anthynus, of course, no "cure" has been necessary in the therapeutic sense; his path has been guided by a supernatural hand, and he receives an earthly crown as a reward for exemplary virtue. For Osriik, the marriage of Anthynus to Queen Bertha and the return of Theodrick have relieved his mind of the antagonism between guilt and passion and, as an acknowledgment of his restored reason, he is betrothed to Mildred. For Offa, no simple resolution is proposed. No one offers the plea Isabella gave for Angelo in *Measure for Measure* that, although evil was intended, the acts never actually materialized. Like most madmen, Offa is under the compulsion to speak the truth so there is no doubt of his guilt even though his intended victims survive. Two possibilities for cure are suggested, however, both of which are in tune with Renaissance religious thought and psychological therapy. First Segebert offers to pray for divine intercession. "His senses," he says, "may bring a new soul into him." Then, as Offa is taken from the stage, Jeffrey, Osriik's fool, volunteers:

> I'll off with him, for 'tis unknown to you
> What good a fool may on a mad man do.[11]
>
> (G 1^v; V,i)

Because they are "penitent" and were "strong instruments" in Mildred's rescue, the outlaws who were part of Offa's schemes are shown mercy; but Offa's future is left open.

No one can fault Brome for his suiting of characterization to the high thematic seriousness of *The Queen's Exchange* nor deny his sincerity in portraying the necessity for adhering to fundamental values, a pre-Caroline concern which remained constant throughout his career. The play also illustrates, however, a weakness which Brome really never overcame. Skillful though he was at comic dialogue, serious speech did not come easily to his pen. Anthynus's moral declamations and

Osriik's wooing of Mildred are stiff and ponderous. Against these, the attempts at comic relief such as the bawdy levity of the fool and the lords are gross and jarring.

The Queen's Exchange also falters structurally. Rather than bringing his characters together mid-play as he does in the comedies, Brome is forced to jump back and forth between Wessex and Northumbria because of the nature of the bifurcated narrative. The result is a series of episodes and there is no unified plot line. Finally, although we may recognize that conventions of tragicomedy which may seem absurd to us were accepted by Renaissance audiences, it is hard to believe that they did not find such contrivances as the mistaken identities of Anthynus and Osriik incredible. Mildred does not even recognize that the king is not her own brother! The coincidence that graverobbers and assassins should emerge from a pit (the outlaws hanging on by the teeth to the buttocks of the robbers) just in time to hide Mildred under their cloaks is an improbability of situation hard to take seriously. Whatever credit Brome deserves for the dramatization of moral psychology is far outweighed by structural ineptness, theatrical contrivances, and contradictions in the laws of cause and effect.

II The Queen and Concubine

During the five years which separate *The Queen's Exchange* (1630–31) from Brome's second tragicomedy, *The Queen and Concubine* (1635–36), he had written *The Novella, The Weeding of Covent-Garden, The Late Lancashire Witches* (with Thomas Heywood), and, perhaps, *The Sparagus Garden.* How much had he learned about writing drama and, in particular, about writing tragicomedy? A great deal. This does not mean that *The Queen and Concubine* achieves the success of Brome's best comedies; it does not. He still is guilty of using an occasional outmoded and stagy theatrical device and he still has trouble with the sustained dialogue of serious emotion. But, as Ronald Bayne points out, in *The Queen and Concubine* "we escape from inflated sentiment and return to a simplicity of moral feelings which belongs to the early days of drama."[12]

The first impression gained from *The Queen and Concubine* is how remarkably akin it is to Shakespearean romantic comedy; how much it is like what Northrop Frye calls "drama of the green world, its plot being assimilated to the ritual theme of the triumph of life and love over the waste land."[13] The action moves from the court world dominated by fortune and the desire for material growth and social advancement to a green world dominated by nature and the desire for spiritual growth and moral advancement. Although the stage action begins earlier in the narrative, Queen Eulalia is somewhat like Duke Senior in *As You Like It*. Both are banished from the court world and become the dominating presence in their own particular green worlds. Eulalia's soliloquy at the beginning of Act III contrasts the external world of fortune with the removed world where natural values are perceived in sentiments similar to those of Shakespeare's exiled Duke. Her answer to her own question, "What's my loss?" makes clear the distinction between what man *thinks* is real and important but is actually false and illusory and what is *true* reality in terms of natural human values:

> I was not great
> Till now; nor could I confidently say
> Any thing was mine own, till I had nothing.
> They do but sleep, that live in highest Pomp;
> And all their happiness is but a dream,
> When mine is real. . . .
>
> (D 6^v; III,i)

The words which follow continue the contrast between seeming and reality but they also dwell upon the rejuvenative powers of the green world and forecast the conversions which bring about the ultimate reconciliation and harmony at the end of the play.

The influence of Divine Providence is much stronger in *The Queen and Concubine* than in the contrived action of *The Queen's Exchange*. It is true that a visionary figure "Genius" is used in both plays and that the use of such a device in the public theater was artificial and outdated by the time Brome was writing *The Queen and Concubine*.[14] Because there is a clearly defined world of romance in the later play, however, the supernatural merges more successfully with the thematic development. The figure of Eulalia has already been established as personifying pure virtue before she lies down to sleep in the fields of Palermo. That she should then be miraculously endowed with superhuman powers to match her superhuman grace and stoicism does not jar the audience's sense of dramatic credibility.[15] Also unlike the earlier play, *The Queen and Concubine* has a strong focus of interest in Eulalia and a clearly developed plot line. Regardless of whether the stage setting at any point in the play is the court world of the Kingdom of Sicily or the pastoral world of Palermo, this play deals with the tribulations and ultimate joys of Queen Eulalia. Like *The Queen's Exchange*, however, the strongest dramatic representation of Brome's moral precepts is again developed through a trichotomy of characters.

The source of the story of "Our Queen," whom Ashley H. Thorndike identifies with the Saint Griselda archetype,[16] is the first tale of *Penelope's Web* by Robert Greene.[17] Although in many ways Brome has remained close to his source, deletions and additions, shifts in emphasis, and, in particular, the highlighting of character enabled the playwright to adapt the prose narrative into a drama of strong moral force. The character of Eulalia and many of the details of the trials of patience she bears are essentially the same as that in the tale told in *Penelope's Web*. The only additions made by Brome are those which emphasize the distinct separation of the court of Sicily and all that it represents from its province of Palermo or, to repeat Frye's terms, the waste land from the green world, and the strong connection between the heroine's virtue and Divine Providence—that force which, emanating through her, brings about the ultimate conversion and rebirth of the wayward characters. The other two principals, Alinda and King Gonzago, however, are dramatically extended far beyond the two-dimensional figures of Greene's didactic little narrative and take symbolic positions somewhat similar to Offa and Osriik in *The Queen's Exchange*.

Olynda (Alinda) in Greene's story is nothing more than a strumpet who seduces the King. Her demands upon him after her elevation to power are ultimately judged as presumptuous ambition and she is banished to "perpetual exile."[18] On the other hand, prior to her appearance at court, Brome's Alinda had lived apart from the intrigues and ambitions which surround Sicily's throne. Eulalia describes the "simple Country innocence" (B 4ᵛ; I,iii) that so delighted her when Alinda first came to keep the Queen company during the King's absence at the wars. Unlike Offa in *The Queen's Exchange*, Alinda's fall from grace is part of the dramatic action. Only *after* she enters the court world do pride and ambition begin to flourish.[19] It is unfortunate that Brome chose to use as contrived a device as a pill administered by a self-seeking servant to cause this change but, nonetheless, the point is made—"She has swallowed an Ambition That will burst her" (B 8[r]; I,vi). Her justification for her receptiveness to the King's advances is indicative of how quickly she learns the ways of court advancement. When her father questions her immoral behavior, she replies:

> Pray Sir
> Let me but ask you this, then use your pleasure:
> (Cause you style Impudence, that which I call Courtship)
> What Courtier sits down satisfied with the first
> Office or Honor is conferred upon him?
> If he does so, he leaves to be a Courtier.
> And not the thing we treat of. Did your self
> After the King had graced you once, twice, thrice,
> (As he kissed me) expect no further from him?

Sforza's amazed reply to this impudence is a telling one:

> She's wondrously well read in Court already:
> Who in the *Devils name* [italics mine] has been her Lecturer?

Her fall is as swift as Eve's, and so is the ease with which she discards past instruction:

> Sovereignty you know, admits no Parentage.
> Honour, poor pretty Honor forgets Descent.
> Let but a silly Daughter of a City
> Become a Countess, and note how squeamishly
> She takes the wind of her Progenitors.
>
> (B 7[v]-8[r]; I,vi)

A distinction can now clearly be made between the *kind* of character Eulalia is and the *kind* Alinda is. Eulalia, we have seen, is constant. She is placed in a set of circumstances which may affect her material condition but does not touch her moral condition. She remains morally inviolate. Alinda, on the other hand, is acted upon and corrupted. The court itself instructed her in the ways of ambition and then Flavello's evil device unnaturally intensified her desire for power and position. It follows, then, that as an *un*natural device increased her moral corruption therefore a *super*natural device—the trance—and the powers of virtue can bring about a moral reawakening. This awakening recalls Eulalia's words, "They do but sleep, that live in highest Pomp; And all their happiness is but a dream" (D 6ᵛ; III,i), and Alinda's words couple this awakening with rebirth:

> How have I wandered in the way of Error!
> Till I was worn into an Airy vapour.
> Then wrapped into a cloud: and thence distilled,
> Into the earth to find a new creation.
> 'Tis found: and I am found in better state,
> Than I was in, before I lost my Duty.
> For in this second Birth: I find a knowledge
> How to preserve it. . . .
>
> (I 8ᵛ; V,ix)

Miraculous salvation is accompanied by the knowledge that she must withdraw from the world which her presence has abused, and she chooses to do this in a nunnery named for Mary Magdalene. If such a miraculous conversion seems incredible, perhaps it might be wise to remember Duke Frederick's meeting with an old religious man in *As You Like It* and how he was "converted Both from his enterprise and from the world."[20] Once the world of romance is accepted, so are the miracles.

The King of Sicily represents still another *kind* of character and is again of much more significance in Brome's play than he is in *Penelope's Web*. For Greene, King Saladyne merely provides the circumstances in which Barmenissa (Eulalia) can prove her virtue. His excuse for turning from his wife is that he has tired of her; "he began to loathe that in the fruit which he loved in the bud."[21] Only after his subsequent actions—the exile of Barmenissa and the decree upon her of poverty, and the crowning of Olynda and his marriage to her—is he described as one whose "immoderate pride and presumption had [in the past] been mitigated by the virtuous clemency of his wife."[22] His change of heart at the end of the Greene tale begins only when Olynda accuses Barmenissa of conspiracy against her life. To test Olynda, he grants her "free liberty to make choice of three things without deny all whatsoever she would crave."[23] Except for the blinding of the former Queen, a demand added by Brome, the concubine's choices are the same in the Greene story as Brome later uses in the play—she would have the lives of the nobles who conspired against her, the disinheritance of the King's son, and the banishment of Eulalia from the realm. The King's response places all the blame on Olynda. *She* is guilty of pride; *she* is presumptuous; *she* would be guilty of unnatural actions; and so on. The story ends:

Olynda falling at the knees of the Souldan would have made reply, but he commanded her to be taken out of his presence, which the Lords performed in all haste: then he sent for his wife, and after reconciliation made, to the great joy of all his Subjects, in lieu of her patient obedience set her in her former state.[24]

In the sequence of events which initiate the action at the beginning of *The Queen and Concubine,* Brome is careful to establish his King as a man easily susceptible to passions. His pride is first shown in his jealousy of his general's reputation. The acclaim which Sforza receives is an injury to the monarch's self-esteem and Eulalia's praise for Sforza leads the King to suspect her of infidelity *before* Alinda catches his eye. Somewhat like Shakespeare's Lear or Leontes, the King in Brome's play is self-infected and, once having his reason distorted by unnatural self-concern, is an easy prey to further whims of passion and excess. The King thus becomes the third member of a triad. Eulalia, in the face of adversity and temptation, remains inviolate; Alinda was acted upon and corrupted and therefore had to be acted upon to be purified; finally, the King is self-infected and, if the pattern holds true, must then grow to self-awareness and self-recognition. And this is just the kind of character Brome tries to give the King.

Gonzago is endowed with certain qualities of royal stature in the opening scenes which provide a norm of reason and justice to which the monarch will return at the end of the play. Even at the moment when he becomes aware of the equal praises heaped by his people upon him and Sforza, Gonzago nonetheless sets this aside and enjoys his blessings:

       The voice
Of the wild people as I passed along

Threw up his praises nearer unto Heaven
Even methought than mine: but be it so,
He has deserved well, now let me again
Embrace the happy comforts of my life.
Through deadly dangers, yea through death itself,
I am restored unto my Heaven on Earth,
My Wife and Son: a thousand blessings on thee.

(B 3ʳ; I,iii)[25]

Again, by implication, the King has been a man to warrant the love and obedience of Eulalia and the unquestioning loyalty of Sforza. Unfortunately, this early image is not strong enough to offset the rapidity with which he falls to jealousy and lust. Brome does not give Gonzago a convincingly strong position from which to fall. By the same token, the language of his grief at the report of his son's death, although intended to reveal natural emotions, is stiff and histrionic. Its strained hyperbole fails to extenuate his previous unnatural treatment of the youth. Only after he is faced with Alinda's madness and a chaotic state, do his responses begin to show a returning to sanity and justice and the process of his growing self-recognition and return to rationality becomes dramatically more skillful.

Event after event is designed to afford him opportunity for acceptance of his own complicity in the chaos which grips the Sicilian court, while at the same time providing effective contrast to the interspersed glimpses of Palermo in which attempts at discord fail to shake the quiet order where Eulalia's virtue reigns. The bravery displayed by the King when "heaps of dangers" surround him during the armed rebellion against Petruccio recalls the triumph acclaimed over his victorious return from the wars in the opening scenes. Affairs of state take precedence over selfish passions. This time he determines to defend Petruccio "more readily" because of the unjust demands he made upon his general's loyalty. The reappearance of Sforza brings on further self-questioning and then a plea for divine aid:

Great Power, that knowest
The subtlety of hearts, show me some light
Through these Cymmerian mists of doubts and fears,
In which I am perplexed even to distraction:
Show me, show me yet the face of glorious Truth;
where I may read

If I have erred, which way I was misled.

(H 4ʳ; IV,viii)

A reconciliation of the monarch with both his generals is
followed by the end of all his doubts as to where true loyalty lies
and a recognition of the intensity of his own error. Mere self-
recognition and the restoration of Queen Eulalia to her former
state are not enough, however, to sustain the strong morality
theme which Brome uses to unify the action of his play. Whereas
Greene says merely that Kings "are Lords o'er Fame and
Fortune,"[26] Brome has added the corollary, but *not* over life,
death, time, and love, nor over holy sacrament. With recognition
of error and repentance must come penance for the violation of
natural and divine law; a penance self-decreed and self-
accepted. Thus the King vows his life "unto the monastry Of holy
Augustinians at *Solante* (K 1ʳ; V,ix) as atonement for unnatural
abuse of his duties as husband, father, and monarch.

The three distinctly different relationships between the
individual and the world which this triad of main characters in
The Queen and Concubine presents are indicative of Brome's
strong moral sense which has about it lingering qualities of a
medieval morality play in which there can be no compromise
between virtue and the temptations of the flesh. There is never
any suggestion that the old court and Palermo can coexist within
a reunited Kingdom of Sicily. The court world must be purged
before the new King can be crowned; the green world must
triumph over the waste land.

No critic could hope to convince the reader that *The Queen
and Concubine* is a great drama or, for that matter, that it comes
anywhere near the dramatic success Brome achieved in his
romantic comedies and satires. Still it is not without merit. Felix
E. Schelling found the conclusion to *The Queen and Concubine*
"creditable to Brome's moral sense."[27] "Brome," says R. J.
Kaufmann, "always remembering the insuperable disparity in
ability, follows Shakespeare's path in *The Queen and Concubine.*"[28] In spite of its lapses, *The Queen and Concubine*
certainly deserves recognition for the Elizabethan quality of
high moral tone which Brome achieves well within the bounds of
tragicomic form and for the implementation of fine character
diversity and thematic unity to support that tone.

CHAPTER 6

Brome as Collaborator

OF five plays with which Richard Brome's name is associated as collaborating author, very little is known. *A Fault in Friendship* is usually assumed to be his first dramatic attempt. The play was entered October 2, 1623, in a lost office-book of the Master of the Revels as having been prepared for the Prince's Company (then performing at both the Curtain and the Red Bull) and written by "*Young* Johnson and Broome." There is, as Bentley points out, no support for the myth that "Young Johnson" was the son of Brome's benefactor.[1] The play has not survived, and nothing is known of it beyond this notice.

Christianetta might also be an early play and might also be a collaboration. An August 4, 1640, entry in the Stationers' Register reads:

Entered for Crooke six Playes vis^t. Christianetta. The Jewish gentleman. A new Academy or Exchange. The love sick Co^{rt}. The Covent Garden. and The English Moore or mock Marriage by M^r. Rich: Broome.

In a list of plays found in the notebook of Abraham Hill (1635–71) the play appears as a collaboration between Richard Brome and George Chapman.[2] If so, Brome may have gained his earliest experience working with George Chapman when the aged Elizabethan dramatist was doing little but collaborating. Considering that Chapman died in 1634 and had written nothing since about 1613, this would suggest a very early date for *Christianetta*, perhaps even before *A Fault in Friendship*. Bentley conjectures that the subtitle given for the play in Hill's list, *Marriage and Hanging Go by Destiny*, sounds like those being produced at the Red Bull around 1623 and 1624.[3] There is also the possibility that Hill was wrong and that *Christianetta* was of Brome's hand alone, in which case it might belong to the 1634–35 period, when he was writing for the Red Bull. Finally *Christianetta* may have been a revision of an earlier Chapman play of which Hill had some manuscript evidence. About *The Jewish Gentleman* in the same entry, nothing is known but the title.

Questions of authorship also arise about the entry in the Stationers' Register for April 8, 1654. It reads:

'Mr. Moseley. Entred for his Copies Two plaies called. The Life and Death of S^r. Martyn Skink. wth ye warres of ye Low Countries. by Rich. Broome & Tho: Heywood. & The Apprentices Prize, &c.'

Greg says it is wrong to assume *The Apprentice's Prize* is a Brome-Heywood collaboration. The plural "plaies" in the Stationers' Register, he claims, can be ignored.[4] It is also possible that the "Two plaies" means *The Life of* and *The Death of Sir Martin Skink* in the same way as there is a *Downfall of* and *Death of Robert, Earl of Huntingdon* or a *Bussy D'Ambois* and a *Revenge of Bussy D'Ambois*. One way or the other, the wording of the entry seems to indicate that *The Apprentice's Prize* was not meant to be ascribed to the two authors named. Of the Martin Skink play(s), nothing is known beyond this entry, but there seems little doubt it was a collaboration of Brome and Heywood. Bentley again suggests that its title sounds like those in vogue at the Red Bull or Fortune rather than a King's Men or Globe play.[5] If this be the case, the collaboration may well have been as early as 1623–24 (which seems unlikely) or as late as 1634–35, after *The Late Lancashire Witches*—after Brome left off his relationship with the King's Men but before he joined the Salisbury Court players.

I   The Late Lancashire Witches

With *The Late Lancashire Witches* we are on firm ground. It is the one extant play for which Brome was a known collaborator. It was printed in 1634 with the names Thomas Heywood and Richard Brome on the title page. Even the earlier controversy as to whether Brome was collaborator with or reviser of Heywood has been settled. Professor R. G. Martin summarizes the contradicting views in his article, "Is *The Late Lancashire*

Witches a Revision?"[6] Martin repeats the results of research done by Professor Wallace Notestein into the witchcraft trials of the period[7] and then takes the position that *"The Late Lancashire Witches* was an entirely new play, the product of the joint authorship of Heywood and Brome, written in 1634."[8] It is not an older Heywood play based on the Lancashire witch trials of 1612 which Brome updated to take advantage of the resurgence of interest in witch-hunting after the later Lancashire trial of 1633. The basis of Martin's argument is the lack of proven parallels to the earlier trial and the direct correlation between the play and the actual depositions recorded in the Calendar of State Papers during the 1633 trials. Professor A. M. Clark's study of Thomas Heywood concurs with Martin and adds such strong additional evidence from the 1633 trial that little doubt can remain that the Brome-Heywood production in 1634 was a new play, an example of dramatic journalism written explicitly to exploit the popular interest.[9]

Clark also suggests it was Richard Brome who initiated the idea for the play. "Brome," he points out, "had been writing for the King's Men for some time before this, and it was probably he who approached the free-lance Heywood, a famous witch-lorist, to assist him in a play on the topic of the moment, the Lancashire witch scare of 1634."[10] In addition, the familiar tri-level plotting of *The Late Lancashire Witches* suggests that the overall structure of the play was Brome's design. The arrangement seems to have worked reasonably well. There is every reason to believe that the two playwrights were compatible despite their differences in age and experience. Both were lovers of the middle-class scene, both were skillful handlers of incident and complicated plot, both had been actors, and both had the practical attitudes of professional playwrights. Heywood, using his experience from *A Woman Killed with Kindness* (1603) and *The English Traveller* (1624), was responsible for the main plot in which the serious aspects of a wife led astray are handled. This time, however, it is the powers of darkness which intrude into the domestic scene. The comic scenes concerning Whetstone and his tormentors are interconnected with the main plot and are also probably Heywood's. Brome, on the other hand, with his experience and skill in farcical comedy, contributed the Seely plot and also may have contributed some of the farcical elements in the witches' scenes. In addition, close reading of the various interconnections between the plots suggests that Brome was responsible for continuity.

The Late Lancashire Witches, then, has three levels of dramatic representation—serious, comic, and farcical. Each, in various degrees from grave to ridiculous, is invaded by the powers of witchcraft. In the main plot, Mrs. Generous, wife to a man of "noble worth"[11] who "ever studied plainness and truth withal" (B 3ᵛ; I,i), has been wooed by the devil into the circle of witches. She and her cohorts are the perpetrators of grave and mischievous deeds which disorder the lives of all others in the play. Interestingly enough, the serious part of the play, the Generous plot, takes the least stage time and is the weakest. In fact, A. M. Clark admits that "when read alongside the vigorous farcical scenes of Brome's contribution it seems slight and lacking in interest." Clark also presents the reason why the situation of the wayward wife falters in this play. "As witchcraft occupies a field debatable in a way unparalleled between tragedy and comedy," he says, "the witch play encourages the introduction of incongruous episodes which weaken the pathos that the essentially tragic situations might produce."[12] The woman unfaithful to her husband, even led to plot against him, usually forms the basis for a domestic tragedy. Yet *The Late Lancashire Witches* is a comedy. Never does the witchcraft actually threaten the lives of the principal characters; there is never a suggestion that it could emerge triumphant over natural forces, and as the play falters to its close, the principals in what might have been a tragic situation emerge as either uninteresting or matter-of-fact and smug.

The comic and farcical parts of the play, however, are lively with interference in otherwise disciplined lives by the undisciplined occult. Heywood's comic Whetstone plot, which involves Mrs. Generous's nephew with three landowners of the area, introduces strange happenings to the audience. Before the opening scene, the three men have been hunting and, right before their eyes, their quarry had suddenly disappeared. No logical explanation will satisfy Master Arthur; accident or chance is not the answer. "But for my part," he says, "I'll hold them prodigies, As things transcending Nature" (B 1ʳ; I,i).

This puzzlement does not distract them from their other game which is baiting the local "Coxcomb," Whetstone, "whom all the brave Blades of the Country use to whet their wits upon"

(B 1^v-2^r; I,i). The poor simpleton takes their taunts, even their accusation that he is a witch, until Bantam oversteps the mark and suggests that rather than "an old wither'd witch," Whetstone's mother was a "young wanton wench." This taunt of bastardy sends Whetstone tattling to his aunt which results in one of Heywood's better scenes (I 1^r-3^r; IV,i). At a banquet to which the baiters have been invited, Mrs. Generous conjures up a series of visions which bear some earmarks of a mock masque. One after the other, a pedant, a tailor, and a groom appear and dance for the guests. During each part of the performance one of the men is singled out as being the performer's natural son. Now the situation is reversed—the usually skilled baiters have become tormented, and the witless Whetstone has the upper hand. Reassurance and the restoration of order come only when the suspicions of supernatural influences are confirmed at the end of the play.

Brome's contribution to *The Late Lancashire Witches*, the Seely plot, provides the most vivid topsy-turvydom in the play and the most startling incongruities. Designed as they are to integrate Brome's farcical invention into the main plot, the lines which first describe the strange reversals within the Seely household are probably Brome's. When Generous wonders why Seely will not stand as security for his nephew's loan, Arthur tells him:

> Because he's late become the sole discourse
> Of all the country; for of a man respected
> For his discretion and known gravity,
> As master of a governed Family,
> The house (as if the ridge were fixed below,
> And groundsils lifted up to make the roof)
> All now turned topsie turvy.

Generous, ironically, refuses to countenance any suspicion of witchcraft even though Arthur describes remarkably strange behavior:

> The good man, in all obedience kneels unto the son,
> He with an austere brow commands his father.
> The wife presumes not in the daughter's sight
> Without a prepared curtsy. The girl, she
> Expects it as a duty; chides her mother

> Who quakes and trembles at each word she speaks;
> And what's as strange, the maid she domineers
> O'er her young mistress, who is awed by her.
> The son to whom the father creeps and bends,
> Stands in as much fear of the groom his man.
> All in such rare disorder, that in some
> As it breeds pity, and in others wonder;
> So in the most part laughter.
>
> (B 4^{r-v}; I,i)

Immediately following these lines, the scene shifts and the audience is treated to a visual representation of what has just been described. This kind of ordering, verbal to visual, suggests that Brome was the architect for the sequence. Indeed, it is characteristic of Brome's method in other plays. In *The City Wit* Crasie describes how he intends to outwit his false friends; this is followed by scenes in which he fulfills his purpose. In *The English Moor*, the circumstances leading up to Quicksands's marriage to Millicent are revealed before their hilarious confrontation on stage.

The Seely plot uses frequent reversals: son over father, groom over son; then daughter over mother, maid over daughter, until, finally, the servants are doing so well by the mixup that they feel they can afford to marry and enjoy their fine things together. Parnell and Lawrence, the servants, soon become the focus of interest in the Seely plot and their highjinks, punctuated by coarse, dialectal language, the main source of bawdy laughter. Though they appear at this point to be favored by the witches, however, they soon become their victims. Lawrence has previously been the love of Mal Spencer, a serving lass turned witch, and it is highly unlikely she shall miss the wedding — though she "care not for the loss of him," she shall not miss the opportunity to "fit" him (E 2^v; II,i). Seely's friend, Doughty, can only stand by and wonder at such goings-on, uttering such expressions as, "This cannot be but witchcraft," "She is most evidently bewitched," and, finally, "Sure all the witches in the Country have their hands in this homespun medley" (C 2^v-3^r; I,i).

At first the Seelys think church bells ringing backwards is but a "merry conceit" (E 3^r; III,i) of the ringers, but when their well-prepared banquet begins to go awry they are totally dumbfounded. Obviously Mal has been at work. First the wedding cake turns to bran; then the leg of mutton in plum broth, the sirloin of beef, and the capon are all transformed in such a way that again Doughty cries, "Witches, live witches, the house is full of witches" (E 4^v; III,i). And indeed it is. Further strange happenings are recounted by Arthur and his friends before the participants sweep back on stage to act out the report of their mad behavior. A counterreversal has come about in the Seely household. The relationship of children and parents has become excessive doting. "They are," says Arthur, "all as far beyond their wits now in loving one another, as they were wide of them before in crossing" (F 2^v; III,i). As for the bridal party, first Parnell wants to go to bed and Lawrence won't, then he wants to and she won't, and "the next minute they both forget they are married." The mad dancing, performed to the strains of musicians all playing different tunes, is only broken for Mal to give her ex-love a "cod-piece point"[13] before the company leaves the stage.

Almost all of Act III is given over to a scene which forms the high point of the farcical plot, if not the entire play, and which displays some of Brome's most successful dramatic techniques. The tempo starts slowly and builds up to a virtual apogee of lawlessness. The dialogue and stage movements move from relatively calm order to disordered frenzy, at first affecting only the Seely menagerie, but ultimately the entire wedding party. To make the scene even more effective in terms of the dramatic totality, he inserts a stop-action interlude in the middle, allowing the audience a brief glimpse of the action in the other two plots. Mrs. Generous is seen bridling her groom and bewitching him to carry her wherever she points, and the three landowners who insulted Whetstone report that he is going to complain to his aunt about them. Each of these incidents leads to further reversals before final order is restored and together they allow the audience (and the actors, we presume) to catch its breath before being swept along toward the approaching crescendo.

Though introduced by lines which sound like Heywood, the witches' scene that follows the wedding charivari is more probably by Brome, for it bears the earmarks of thematic and structural paralleling in his other plays. It also provides a comic foil for the preceding scene in which what should have been order has come to strange disorder in the Seely household. Brome then presents an orderly witch party in which their ability to "pull for" the various dishes that disappeared from the wedding banquet is taken as matter-of-course. The witches chat over their purloined repast as amicably as if they were at a polite social gathering. There are no wild dances but rather a "merry round"; "pair and pair" they "nimbly foot it" (G 2ᵛ; IV,i). In the one, then, a well-ordered wedding turns into a charivari, and in the other the expected confusion of necromantic revels is ordered and moderate.

Although by this time the audience is caught up in the progression of the Seely farce, the coauthors put into motion still another cycle of action. A grave conversation between Generous and his wife is followed by laughing gossip from Arthur, Doughty, and the others of the further problems facing Lawrence and Parnell. Their wedding night has proved a dismal failure. "It seems," Shakestone reports, "the bridegroom was unprovided of" (H 3ʳ; IV,i). This they wonder about, for Lawrence had been known as "an over mickle man among the maids." Doughty again provided the answer:

Witchery, witchery, more witchery still flat and plain witchery. Now do I think upon the codpiece point the young jade gave him at the wedding: she is a witch, and that was a charm, if there be any in the World.

(H 3ʳ; IV,i)

During their conversation, offstage shouts and drums indicate the approach of a "Skimington."[14] Again paralleling the increasing tempo of the action, the sound effects get louder and louder until Lawrence and Parnell burst upon the stage caterwauling bawdy accusations at each other, followed by the Skimington itself. The stage directions indicate that the authors want total hysteria to reign:

Enter drum (beating before) a Skimington, and his wife on a horse; Diverse country rustics (as they pass) Par. (pulls Skimington off the horse: and Law. Skimington's wife: they beat them. Drum beats alar. horse comes away: the hoydens at first oppose the Gentlemen: who draw: the clowns vail[15] bonnet (make a ring Par. and Skim. fight.

(H 4ᵛ; IV,i)

After this progressively gathering momentum, the rest of Act IV is a process of unwinding. The witches' performance put on by

Mrs. Generous in revenge for insult to Whetstone is entertaining but less noisy and bawdy; a rather quiet speech from Mrs. Generous as to how she and her sister-spirits will next move against Generous ends the act. This winding down continues through to the end of the play. With the exception of one frenzied and unsuccessful attempt on the part of the sorcerers to disorder the Generous estates, the last act is taken up with a series of discoveries as natural law emerges triumphant over necromantic law. It is also in Act V that the play falters. Within the bounds of necromantic credibility, the comic Whetstone reversals and the farcical Seely frenzy are explained and set aright. The main plot, on the other hand, creates problems in dramaturgy which Heywood does not succeed in overcoming.

Mrs. Generous's confession that she is a witch comes immediately after she has returned from riding her poor bedeviled groom about the countryside, and at this point the play begins to take on a truly serious tone. Earlier, Generous had been briefly concerned over various unfunny matters: the signing of a security bond, the leasing of his mill, his dislike of his wife's riding out alone. Each of these had been caused by strange circumstances: the topsy-turvy house of the man who should have guaranteed the loan, the original lessee of the mill attacked by unseen beings, the strangeness of his wife's recent behavior. Mrs. Generous's confession (H 1^{r-v}; IV,i) gives her husband the opportunity to recite the superstitions surrounding the fate of one who countenances the devil.

Her desire to repent, so terse as to be unbelievable to anyone but Generous himself, is soon shown to be a sham to fool her husband.

> Some passionate words [she tells one of her underlings],
>   mixed with forced tears,
> Did so enchant his eyes and ears,
> I made my peace, with promise never
> To do the like; but once and ever
> A Witch thou know'st. Now understand
> New business we took in hand.
> My husband packed out of town,
> Know that the house and all's our own.
>
> (I 1^{r}; IV,i)

The witches and their attendant spirits, however, meet their match in the retired soldier turned miller. When they gather to plague him as they had done his predecessor, he beats them off with his sword, his "Good Morglay. . .Comrague[16] and Bedfellow" (K 1^r; V,i). "Fast or loose, most sure I made them fly, And skip out of Port-holes," he reports to Generous, and adds, "But the last I made her squeak . . . There's one hath paid the reckoning" (K 2^r-3^r; V,i). The "last" was Mrs. Generous and the "reckoning" was her hand which the soldier cut off in the mêlée. This rather macabre proof is enough for Generous, and he turns his wife and her cohorts over to the law.

There might be some justification for the shock value, even in a comedy, of a severed hand being passed about onstage. This is not really the problem at the end of *The Late Lancashire Witches*. The play is, after all, relying on audience familiarity with an actual arrest and trial, and with the disposition of Mrs. Generous would come all the implications of what would happen to her and the rest of her cult after their arrest if they were a part of the real world. The laughter engendered by the Whetstone plot and the ridiculous antics of the Seely family tends to dwindle off into rather an ominous silence and the illusion falters. A very serious kind of reality is thrust upon the audience when they have not been prepared for it, and it is in no way parallel or sequential to the other actions.

This flaw and others have their basis in thematic imbalance among the various levels of representation. The farcical elements outweigh the comic, and the comic, in turn, outweigh the serious. A. W. Ward's complaint that the authors "were far too anxious to create an immediate effect to attempt more than a succession of grotesque scenes, vivaciously enough written (partly in what represents the Lancashire dialect), but contemptible as composing a dramatic action,"[17] is only partly justified. The unity of this play is based on connections inherent within cyclical changing tempos, thematic repetition on various levels, and comic reversals. It is obvious that the various plot reversals are cleverly paralleled, as each is suited to a particular level of the plot. The consequences of lawless powers taking over from rational benevolence in Generous *could* have grave and even disastrous results; the turnabout of roles in the Whetstone plot allows the witless to hold sway over the wits; and, most successfully, Brome's Seely plot provides the madcap chaos where everything is upside-down. Structurally and thematically, then, there is a unified dramatic action and, for the farcical and comic levels, a perfectly adequate resolution and reconciliation. Unfortunately, their resolutions depend upon the Generous plot, for which there may be resolution but not reconciliation. Society must be purged of the powers of darkness, not reconciled to them. Thus Heywood is faced with an insurmountable problem—how to hold his serious plot within the bounds of a play in which comic elements have outweighed serious and in which the main stage action has been the results of occult whims, not the reality of necromancy. Somewhat ironically, then, *The Late Lancashire Witches,* a play based upon a real situation, fails at the end because of the intrusion of too much reality. In rather typical Bromean fashion, it is the Seely plot which provides whatever harmony and order are restored at the end of the play. The witches and Whetstone are banished from the stage, which was all that *could* have happened to them. It remains for Brome, then, to reaffirm the positive forces of reconciliation and social order.

CHAPTER 7

Generic Inversion: "The Choice Dainties of His Theatre"

TOWARD the end of his career, Richard Brome wrote three plays each quite different from the others in tone and structure and in which the action takes place in distinctly different settings from any of his other comedies—*The Love-sick Court*, a play which is difficult to date but probably belongs to the late 1630s, *The Antipodes* (1638), and *A Jovial Crew* (1641). In each case, the setting is an integral part of the total effect and gives rise to a specific dramatic situation. Each exposes misconceptions of life directly related to the London theater audience and those playwrights who catered to it. What is more important in these plays and what links the three together is that each achieves its dramatic totality by Brome's turning of the generic form upon itself. *The Love-sick Court* is a parody on romantic tragicomedy; *The Antipodes*, a satire within a satire; and *A Jovial Crew*, an antiromance.

I The Love-sick Court

It seems impossible now that *The Love-sick Court* could ever have been taken as a serious tragicomedy. Yet Swinburne condemned it as "such an example of unromantic romance and unimaginative invention as too often wearies and disappoints the student of English drama in its first period of decadence."[1] Later, Alfred Harbage commented, "Brome . . . became the chief spokesman of professional antagonism toward the courtly invasion and the Cavalier mode. Once, however, he weakened and paid the new fashion the tribute of imitation."[2] In recent years, R. J. Kaufmann's view of the play has superseded these pejorative opinions. He proves that *The Love-sick Court* is not an

118

inept imitation of popular court drama but a burlesque, a romantic parody.[3] As Douglas Sedge points out, the fact "that Brome's play has only recently been recognized as a parody of the courtly mode is perhaps an indication of the degree of hyperbolical magnanimity to be found in the 'straight' courtier plays. Brome is scarcely exaggerating."[4]

Once *The Love-sick Court* is accepted as burlesque, the title itself becomes dual in its implications. Not only is the court of Thessaly "love-sick," but so is the court of Caroline London, which indulges in neo-Platonic games of love and self-love. By the same token, Brome's prologue becomes a satiric thrust at the cavalier playwrights who catered to this self-indulgence.

> *Sometimes at poor men's boards the curious find*
> *'Mongst homely fare, some unexpected dish,*
> *Which at great tables they may want and wish.*
>
> (F 7ʳ)

In the plays discussed in Chapter 4, Brome exposed the folly of the Platonic social fashion and those who would imitate it; in *The Love-sick Court* he strikes at the court plays which dramatically reenact social extravagances and at the dramatists who provide stage mirrors for their devotees—those court playwrights whom a contemporary, James Howell, mocks: "This love sets the Wits of the Town on work. . . ."[5]

The basic narrative structure of *The Love-sick Court* is the simplest of any Brome comedy; it has a main plot concerned with the members of the Thessalonian court and a subplot about their servants. By the laws of Thessaly, should a king be without male issue, the nobleman to whom he would match his daughter becomes "immediate heir to the Crown" (G 1ᵛ; I,i). The nobleman may be a soldier who has done great service to the state, like Stratocles, *The Ambitious Politique* of the subtitle, or "the son of some Great General slain in battle for his country," in this case either of the twins Philocles or Philargus. Princess Eudina must decide in five days or the choice will be turned over to the Commons. Such as it is, the plot potential is in the romantic tradition of *The Knight's Tale* and *The Two Noble Kinsmen*. The complications expected of rival suitors—Philocles-Philargus versus Stratocles—and of rival brothers—Philocles versus Philargus—might be expected in any early Tudor romance.

However, with hilarious abandon, Brome throws in almost every other romantic gimmick imaginable. There is an oracular riddle from Delphi designed to befuddle and confuse the court and the "Twins in birth":

> *Contend not for the Jewel, which*
> *Ere long shall both of you enrich.*
> *Pursue your Fortune: For 'tis she*
> *Shall make you what you seem to be.*
>
> (G 6ʳ; I,ii)

The conundrum gives rise to exaggerated declarations of love and loyalty from each brother to the other. Add to this a dream vision in which Eudina sees Philocles and Philargus embrace and then face each other with swords. Any disappointment that a duel does not ensue is made up for by a mock duel in Act IV when *"they espy one another, draw, and pass at each other, instantly both spread their arms to receive the wound"* (K 1ʳ; IV,ii). When this fails to eliminate one of the brothers, each tries to kill himself. Into this confusion Brome puts a potpourri of suspected incest (Placilla, the twins' sister, agonizes over the illicit love she feels for Philocles); attempted rape, as Stratocles decides seducing Eudina will secure his royal ambitions; and a smattering of humors figures: Stratocles, the braggart soldier; Garrula, a drunken nurse; her son, a pedant whose every utterance is illustrated by the classical "once upon a time"; and a few pastoral rustics who effect some remarkable reversals in character. The playwright also introduces lot-drawing and sleeping potions, miraculous conversions for the villains, a mock funeral procession for Philargus, who rises out of his coffin at the crucial moment, and, finally, the revelation of mistaken identities. Philocles turns out to be the King's son and brother to Eudina, which puts him out of contention for her hand and free for Placilla; Philargus is then the logical mate for the Princess. Professor Kaufmann refers specifically to the mock duel scene, but his remark, "It does not take much visual imagination to see how ludicrous this could be made in the acting,"[6] could take in this whole burlesque.

To add to the absurdity and emphasize the parody, Brome provides a subplot which directly parallels the main one and is deliberately designed to undercut it in manner and motive. Brome's device here is to allow the servants' common sense

continually to cut across the affectations of the courtly circle.
Eudina's maid, Doris, has several suitors: Tersulus and Varillus,
servants to Philargus and Philocles; Geron, the "whilom"
pedant; and Matho, Stratocles's man. The latter two boasters are
caricatured for their pretensions to the courtly extravagances of
the main plot. The first, quite harmless, addresses Doris by
letter. She reads:

> My *Lesbia*, my *Cinthia*, my *Licoris*
> Or (which is best of names) my lovely *Doris*—that's I.
> I still am thine and cannot commutate,
> I am as certain to thee as thy fate.
> 'Tis not my study, or my travails can
> Make me to thee appear another man:
> Thou may'st affirm of me as *Whilom* did
> *Xantippe* of her husband whom she chid,
> Grave *Socrates* regardless of his worth
> He still returned the same as he went forth.
> Before I visit thee, thus may'st thou hear on
> Thine in the tribulation of love —*Geron*.

Her response is, "Fate deliver me" (G 7ᵛ; II,i). Matho's advances
are colored with the same ambitions as his master's, and his
attempt at wooing by circumlocution becomes nonsense:

> I will acquaint my Lord; who for your care
> Shall upon his advancement to the Crown
> Give me command, who will give present order
> Unto my man for your promotion.
>
> (G 8ᵛ; II,i)

Matho's position in the play is that of mock villain and that of
Geron is fool (perhaps together representing the dual nature of
Stratocles). The two serious contenders, Tersulus and Varillus,
"as deeply vow'd in friendship" as are Philargus and Philocles,
each try to woo for the other. Doris finally proposes that she
shall choose the servant of whichever lord Eudina weds, but not
before each servant's apparently selfless dedication to his
brother's suit renders the friendship code of the main plot even
more ludicrous. Only when the glib-tongued Doris drops a hint
for a practical solution does any hope for breaking the stalemate
appear. She affirms her proposition and adds:

> Yes and hold you
> This for Creed, That heaven must make its choice
> Of one of them before she take the other.
> You understand me; and now cease your strife;
> When the one's Lord's dead, I'll be the other's wife.
>
> (I 8^{r-v}; IV,i)

One of the lords must die before either plot can be resolved. To solve the dilemma of a mock romance, however, a mock death and a mock funeral and the revelation of a mock secret leads the play to its conclusion. We are left to visualize what kind of masque dances the actors would devise for Geron, the ruffian-rustics, and for the "Nymphs" (wherever they came from), to end the play on a final hilarious note.

The Love-sick Court is a credit to Brome's ingenuity. It is the only time that he actually invades and stays in the court world[7] and, by deliberately breaking in upon the domain of the dramatists whom he had condemned for misconstruing the aims of comedy,[8] he successfully ridicules their world and their art.

II   The Antipodes

Although *The Love-sick Court* is highly stylized and triumphant in its mockery, *The Antipodes* is the most sophisticated and ingenious of Brome's satires. In this play he uses a dramatic framework specifically adapted to a particular satiric intent, based upon the idea of an antipodal London. Unlike the plays using place-realism, *The Antipodes* has a hypothetical rather than an actual setting through which the characters in the play (and the audience to it) recognize their follies and the follies of London life by observing their opposites in a kind of distorted mirror. The effect is as if the audience were standing with its back to a large mirror and seeing what is reflected in it over its shoulder by using a second mirror held in the hand.

In the opening scene, Joyless, an old country gentleman, has brought his son to Doctor Hughball in London to be cured of a melancholic madness brought on by excessive reading of extravagant travel books.[9] Peregrine Joyless has totally withdrawn from the world of reality into an illusory world filled with phantasmagoria and unnatural natural science. The psychiatrist Hughball lives with "a phantastic Lord," Letoy, and together they form a director-producer relationship for a play-within-a-play through which a comic catharsis takes place and the young man is cured. *The Antipodes* is a "dramatization of psychiatric therapy"[10] which, with the possible exception of Ford's *The Lover's Melancholy* (1628), is unparalleled in Renaissance drama.[11]

Hughball's psychiatric method, the basic comic device of the play, is ingenious in its simplicity. The doctor presumes the young man to be quite sane and offers to transport him to the most distant of all Sir John Mandeville's exotic places—the "world of *Antipodes*," where the people

> In outward feature, language, and religion,
> Resemble those to whom they are supposite:
> They under *Spain* appear like *Spaniards,*
> Under *France Frenchmen,* under *England English*
> To the exterior show: but in their manners,
> Their carriage, and condition of life
> Extremely contrary.
>
> (C 4ʳ; I,vi)

Hughball whets the characters' anticipation with a description of the antipodal world where "contrary to us . . . people rule the Magistrates," "men do all the tittle-tattle duties while women Hunt, Hawk, and take their pleasure." Antipodean women hunt falcons with pheasant, deer pursue hounds, and cats are kept in cages to protect them from mice; lords sell their belongings to feast their servants, and "Merchants wives do deal abroad Beyond the seas, while their husbands cuckold them At home." Lawyers are honest men who work at trades during vacations so they may "give the law for nothing in the term times"; the clergy, on the other hand, are covetous court wranglers. "Hirelings, clowns, and tradesmen" enjoy "all wit and mirth and good society" while poets and players are Puritans (C 4ʳ-D 1ᵛ; I,vi). After these and other examples, the verbal becomes visual. At the beginning of Act II, Peregrine awakens from a drugged sleep actually believing he has slept for eight months and has traveled to antipodal London. Acts II, III, and IV are given over to the play-within-the-play performed by Letoy's servants for the benefit of Peregrine and in which he is the central character. Hughball's examples also prepare the theater audience for life in topsy-turvydom, and once what Swinburne called the "incongruous congruity of contradictions"[12] is accepted, every antipodal sequence follows with superbly logical and hilarious consistency.

The scheme offers infinite possibilities covering a comic spectrum ranging from burlesque farce (such as two "catchpoles" running away from a gentleman who wants to be arrested) to the subtlest satire. Consider, for example, the satiric perambulations of a gentleman brought to court for refusing to sleep with the wife of a merchant from whom he has received various wares. The gentleman not only refuses to pay double for the wares but declares virtuously he wishes to "content" only his wife. The merchant's argument is in the form of an elaborate progression of logic: tradesmen live off gentlemen; gentlemen content women; contented women make good wives; tradesmen need good wives; even if a tradesman shall consume the gentleman's estate, his son (through the contented wife) shall ultimately inherit it anyhow. Therefore, the gentleman should sleep with the merchant's wife. Letoy's servant, who plays the part of the judge, gives a qualified verdict. As a Justice, he should make an example of the gentleman and deny him the sight of any woman until he give satisfaction to the merchant's wife so that such a dangerous breach of custom does not occur again. But as he is "a Citizen by nature" he will use "urbanity." Finally, he concludes,

> And as I am a gentleman by calling,
> (For so my place must have it) I'll perform
> For you the office of a gentleman
> Toward his wife, I therefore order thus:
> That you bring me the wares here into Court
> (I have a chest shall hold them, as mine own)
> And you send me your wife, I'll satisfy her
> My self. I'll do it, and set all straight and right:
> Justice is blind, but Judges have their sight.
>   (G 4^{r-v}; III,viii)

Peregrine is so impressed with such a display that he knights By-Play on the spot. In a single scene, Brome attacks all the social, economic, and legal abuses which he has exposed in other plays, although never so compactly, so pointedly, or so humorously.

An equal credit to Brome's dramatic skill is the manner in

which he prevents sequence after sequence of cloud-cuckoo reversals from losing their comic impact. In the first place, Peregrine is not the only one suffering from a fixation malady. His wife, Martha, still a virgin after three years of marriage because her husband prefers the pleasures of fantasy to those of the nuptial couch, is in a frenzy of child-longing. Secondly, Old Joyless, partnered in a January-May second marriage, suffers from irrational jealousy toward his young wife, Diana. These three, with Letoy, are the important onstage spectators to the play-within-the-play,[13] and their comments upon the action cut across the absurd contraries of the antipodal world, keeping the theater audience constantly aware of the various levels of representation.

At the end of Act IV, Peregrine, having been convinced Martha has been transformed into a Princess of the Antipodes, kisses her and they retire to a bedchamber. The "real knowledge of a woman," prophesies Letoy, will be the last step of his remedy. By degrees "his much troubled and confused brain" will become "settled and rectified" (K 1ʳ; IV,xii). The consummation also cures Martha's concern for her untouched maidenhead and implies that she will not be childless for long.

All but the last sequence is then given over to curing Joyless of his jealousy. For this Brome introduces another play-within-a-play, this one to be produced for Joyless. In this sequence Letoy is a conscious actor, Diana an unconscious participant, and Joyless the concealed observer. When Diana's chastity remains indignantly firm before Letoy's mock persuasions, Joyless is convinced of the strength of her purity and the folly of his jealousy.

Still another kind of performance is inserted within the greater play in the last scene, a moral masque that celebrates the triumph of Harmony over Discord. The antimasque, in which Discord's factions, Folly, Jealousy, Melancholy, and Madness hold the stage, represents the previous joylessness of those who were her victims. Then Letoy signals the approach of the main masquers:

> See Harmony approaches, leading on,
> 'Gainst Discord's factions, four great dieties;
> *Mercury, Cupid, Bacchus,* and *Apollo.*
> Wit against Folly, Love against Jealousy,
> Wine against Melancholy, and 'gainst Madness, Health.
>
> (L 4ʳ; V,xi)

Discord is, of course, confounded by the forces of Harmony in Letoy's masque as surely as it was in his playlet for Joyless and in his master production for Peregrine, and the play ends with Peregrine's epilogue to the audience asking for their "gentler hands" to dispel that last of their fears. Thus as Letoy, the doctor within the play-world, cures his patients, so Brome the doctor-playwright hopes to cure his theater audience through comic catharsis.

Various suggestions have been made for sources of *The Antipodes,* particularly for the device of a play-within-a-play as a cure for some character's malady.[14] Rather than being related to any other specific production, *The Antipodes* more likely falls within the tradition of plays which include interpolated interludes, plays, or masques for some dramatic revelation.[15] More important speculations have been made as to the invention of reversal. Joe Lee Davis would link *The Antipodes* with *The Muse's Looking Glass* (1630) written by another "son of Ben," Thomas Randolph.[16] Randolph's highly artificial play represents Thalia, the muse of Comedy, as having a mirror in which "Vices of Excess and Defect" are made to see their opposites; its characters are allegorical and its aim is a defense of comedy against Puritan attacks on the stage rather than a satire on London life. Another possibility might be William Strode's *The Floating Island,* which was performed first at Cambridge in August 1636. Here the "floating island," England, falls into confusion and disorder when the subject courtiers, represented as various human passions, rebel against their kingly master, Prudentius. Although characters in Strode's play, particularly Sir Amorous and Sir Timerous-Fearall, have a certain quality of Jonsonian humor, the whole production smacks of a kind of university erudition that Brome was more likely to attack than to copy.[17]

Professor Ian Donaldson has shown quite clearly that the notion upon which *The Antipodes* is based belongs within an ancient folk tradition quite familiar to Brome's audience. "So usual was the association of the antipodes with absurdity," he states, "that by Brome's day the phrase *to act the antipodes* had become a proverbial expression for a reversal of the expected order of things."[18] Donaldson draws evidence for the antiquity of the antipodal notion from Cosmas Indicopleustes, the eighth- or ninth-century Greek navigator whose conviction that there was no "antipodes" was based on the improbability of a people who "contrary to nature" existed "head downward."[19] The possibilities for ludicrousness such as this, however, are inherent within the antipodal concept itself, regardless of what Brome's immediate impulse may have been. In fact, Professor Donaldson also shows that the notion of an antipodes is but a part of the whole concept of comic inversion, one metaphoric aspect of a world upside-down.[20]

Other early seventeenth-century works such as Bacon's nondramatic *Nova Atlantis* or Jonson's masque *Newes from the New World Discover'd in the Moon* might also be included as influencing *The Antipodes*. Certain physical similarities between Bacon's fantasy world and Brome's might indicate that the playwright had some knowledge of the *Nova Atlantis* (pub. 1627). The island of Bensalem, according to the opening paragraph of Bacon's unfinished work, was somewhat north of the South Sea route between Peru and the Orient; geographically, the people of the island were closer to being antipodal to those of Great Britain than the people of other fantasy worlds which preceded Brome's. Technical though this may sound, this physical distance achieves the same kind of separation for Bacon as Brome later relied upon in *The Antipodes*—a separation which allows the audience the very objectivity the playwright is seeking. The people of Bacon's fictitious island, however, are allegorical as well as satirical and are certainly much more learned than Brome's Antipodeans. In addition, the people Peregrine thinks he is ruling are not perversions or purified versions of the stage and theater audience but opposites, different by virtue of geography and therefore acceptably different in custom and manner. This very dichotomy of behavior patterns is the basis of Brome's satire.

Although it was not published until the 1641 Folio, there seems to be little doubt that Richard Brome would have known Jonson's *News from the New World Discovered in the Moon,* as he was already associated with the London theatrical world during the time of its writing and production (1620). The geographical setting for Jonson's work, however, bears no resemblance whatsoever to his protégé's antipodal realm. The news of the "Lunatic" world has arrived by "Moonshine" and is reported from the stage at Whitehall by the poet's heralds who also serve as presenters of the masquers and antimasquers.

Nonetheless, some Jonsonian influence in *The Antipodes* lies in specific ideas which Brome may have picked up from the masque dialogue. At one point, after one of the heralds has explained that "Lunatic language" is "only by signs and gestures," he is asked, "How do their Lawyers then?" The conversation continues:

2 Her. They are Pythagorians, all dumb as fishes, for they have no controversies to exercise themselves in.
Fac. How do they live then?
1 Her. On the dew of the Moon like Grasshoppers, and confer with the Doppers [anabaptists].
Fac. Ha' you Doppers?
2 Her. A world of Doppers! but they are as lunatic persons, walkers only, that leave only to hum, and ha, not daring to prophesy, or start up upon stools to raise doctrine.[21]

There is no doubt that Brome's *The Antipodes* is also infused with Jonson's comic vision through which, as Donaldson says, "Folly and wickedness are expressed in terms of moral contrariness." Although this kind of "strong moral polarity"[22] is particularly clear in Brome's "triumph of Harmony over Discord" performance, it is also basic to the whole dramatic representation of the play.

Finally, it must be recognized that although Brome relies upon a familiarity with the concept of antipodeanism, his *dramatic* invention is surely his own. He had experimented with the device before. Less elaborate reversals occur in *The Damoiselle* and in *The City Wit*. The relationship of the Salewares in *A Mad Couple Well Match't* is exactly the case brought before Justice By-Play enacted in its vicious circle of immorality and greed. The most important of his early plays which illustrate this comic technique is surely *The Late Lancashire Witches*, in which the Seely plot provides a visual expression of the necromantic perpetrations which turn the dramatic world quite literally upside-down. In *The Antipodes*, however, the poet uses no magic; no witches play at bowls with normal custom except insofar as Hughball and the playwright himself are witchdoctors. With the same kind of logical consistency that Swift later achieves in *Gulliver's Travels*, but with none of the Swiftian viciousness, Brome provides what Swinburne called a "delicious inversion of all social or natural relations between husband and wife, mistress and servant, father and son, poet and puritan, lawyer and client, courtiers and clowns, [which] might satisfy the most exacting socialist; and the projects for the relief, encouragement, and support of criminals and scoundrels in general at the expense of the State could hardly be held unworthy of consideration by the latest and loudest apostles of professional philanthropy."[23]

Brome proves the value of comic catharsis. His satiric effect is gained by a duality of representation—one assumed to be firm and constant as the viewers' conception of what life is and the other the exaggerations, the opposites, or what they actually see in performance on stage. The catharsis comes through the ultimate realization that what they think and what they see are two distorted reflections of the same vision, and thus comic catharsis within the interpolated performances onstage becomes catharsis for the audience to the greater play. *The Antipodes* is more sophisticated in its manner and method than any other of Brome's comedies and is rivaled only by *A Jovial Crew* in the continued critical praise given it. In fact, the two plays outrank all but the best of Jonson.

III   A Jovial Crew

A Jovial Crew, or *The Merry Beggars,* was first produced in April 1641[24] and, we assume from the dedicatory letter to Thomas Stanley in the 1652 edition, it also *"had the luck to tumble last of all in the* Epidemical *ruin of the* Scene" for the King and Queen's Young Company before the Phoenix in Drury Lane went dark in September 1642, and the greatest age of English drama came to an end. Its pre-Commonwealth stage history lasted a mere sixteen months; from that period there is nothing to indicate with what enthusiasm, if any, it was received. Twenty years later, when it was revived in 1661 by the King's Company at the Vere Street Theatre, four performances in six months[25] attest to a popularity which continued through the seventeenth and eighteenth centuries.[26]

Samuel Pepys's reaction to the play when he saw its first Restoration performance is particularly interesting, as it indicates what has been a continuing audience and critical assessment well into this century. "To the Theatre," says Pepys for July 25, 1661, "and saw 'The Jovial Crew' (the first time I saw it); and indeed, it is as merry, and the most innocent play that ever I saw, and well performed."[27] Intrigued and delighted by its surface romanticism, critics have continued to take at face value the woodland setting in which most of the vagabond action takes place. Even J. A. Symonds exempts *A Jovial Crew* from his critical attack on Brome's works. He admits the plot is "novel" and then goes on to relate it to the *"ecole buissoniere* of existence—which is so strong a characteristic of the English."[28] "Brome turns away from the town" for *A Jovial Crew,* say Professors Thomas Marc Parrott and Robert Hamilton Ball more recently, and "a fresh breath of country air blows through the playhouse while the story of good Squire Oldrents and his merry daughters is unrolled."[29]

This last comment must certainly give the modern reader pause. How fresh is the air which blows through Oldrents's house? Having heard a fortuneteller prophesy that both his daughters, in spite of all his wealth, shall be beggars, he is full of melancholy and grief. His jovial friend Hearty would induce him to count his blessings and be mirthful, but forced merriment is sadder than melancholy. And what of his daughters? Just when are Rachel and Meriel "merry"? Certainly not at the beginning of the play, when they are "pent up and tied by the nose to the continual steam of hot Hospitality" (D 2^r; II,i) in their father's house; when they feel that by contrast to the freedom of the beggars housed in the barn, they are imprisoned by their father's sadness. And what of Springlove, Oldrents's steward, whom he loves as he loves his daughters? Each year there stirs in Springlove's heart and blood the longing to take to the open road, to join the merry crew of vagabonds who frequent the area, but, at the same time, he is aware of a duality of existence which draws him in different directions. It is exactly upon these polarities of existence, symbolized in Springlove, that the fundamental irony of *A Jovial Crew* is based, an irony which is visualized in the dichotomies of the setting and felt in the shifting tone and uneasy mood of the play. Thus, while it is easy to accept that *A Jovial Crew* is certainly different in setting and predisposition from others of Brome's plays, it is more difficult to accept that, at this late stage in his career, a playwright whose forte is obviously satire would turn to escapist drama, to an exultation of a mirthful green world totally divorced from the realities of human experience. By the same token, where we might accept R. J. Kaufmann's view that quite contrary to what previous critics have said, *A Jovial Crew* "is virtually a social parable for the times," it is difficult to see a drama in which song and dance play such a large part as "full of weary disenchantment and something almost like despair for reasonable solutions of real social problems."[30]

Each of the main characters in *A Jovial Crew* turns for various reasons to the company of the merry beggars. Springlove, in answer to his "nature" and in the hope of solving his master's fortune in a literal sense, agrees to effect the escape of Oldrents's daughters into the *"Beggars* Commonwealth" and act as their servant. With them go the ladies' suitors, who, though doubtful that the adventure is to be anything more serious than "a mad trick of youth," decide they must go or lose their loves. On hearing they are gone, Oldrents determines to turn grief to "jovial Mirth" with such vehemence that even Hearty worries, "This is over-done. I do not like it" (F 2^r; II,i). In an effort verging on desperation, then, all leave the external world which they assume is full of care, enforced order, and human responsibility to find a free life among the "only happy People in a Nation" (E 1^r; II,i) in the woodland glade nearby. When Oldrents joins the company of beggars, he expresses their attitudes toward what he sees as the old life and the new,

> What is an estate
> Of Wealth and Power, balanced with their Freedom,
> But a mere load of outward complement?
> When they enjoy the Fruits of rich Content?
> Our Dross but weighs us down into Despair,
> While their sublimed spirits dance in the Air.
>
> (F 3^{r-v}; II,i)

Ironically, it is the reality of the beggar life itself which cuts harshly across the romantic optimism of the escapists. While Oldrents rhapsodizes on the delight of rebirth into a natural world, a beggar doxy's cries in childbirth cut through the "confused noise . . . of laughing and singing." If the folly of the main characters in their attempt to divorce reality from life in order to follow birdsong is not clearly evident to the reader by this point in the play (near the end of Act II), the violent dichotomy between kind, benevolent nature and harsh, painful nature brings it home with stunning impact. The beggars may be "Free above Scot-free; that observe no Law, Obey no Governor, use no Religion, But what they draw from their own ancient custom" (E 1ʳ; II,i), but they are not free from those laws of nature which separate men from "sublimed spirits." For Oldrents, the confrontation with the Patrico's drunken wife and the beggar-priest's offer to provide him with a "Doxie[31] or a Dell[32] that never yet with man did Mell,"[33] takes him aback. "A sudden qualm over-chills my stomach," he responds to Hearty but then, bolstering his determination, "But 'twill away" (G 1ʳ; II,i).

For the young lovers the confrontation with reality is kept in a lighter vein but, nonetheless, their disillusionment is also physical. Their first night of freedom had been anything but tranquil. "Lightening and Tempest," "the noise of the *Crew,*" "the hogs in the Hovel," are not at all what the knights errant expected and their fair damsels are "crupper-crampt," "bumsidled with the straw," "numm'd i' the bum" (G 2ʳ–3ʳ; III,i) from their hard lodging. Where now is the fanciful dream of the free and open road?

And so it goes—begging to eat is not fun but a profession in which hungry days come before the art is learned; the woodland is not free from predators like Oliver, who assumes the girls' virtue is as free as their life appears to be; man does not cast off miserlinesss or selfishness on a whim but carries it with him as does Martin, who agrees to help Amie escape an enforced marriage purely to advance his own station. It would appear that one by one each of the expected triumphs of the green world over the waste land is undercut by intruding a kind of harsh reality into the merry beggars' world.

Equally as skillful as he undercuts romantic notion, Brome also shows the other side of the coin. The hospitality which so marks the beggar-crew is paralleled by Oldrents's open door and, as his name indicates, his charity toward those on his land is as great as theirs under the sky.[34] He is as willing to grant freedom of will to Springlove as the beggar-priest, Patrico, is to his band. Oldrents's concern for his daughters' happiness and future would cast him as the genuine Patrico and the beggar-priest's vulgar disregard for anything more than the physical functions of the "doxies" and "dells" as somewhat obscene. Justice Clack may be a fool but he is harmless compared to the immorality of the lawyer-beggar or the soldier-beggar. The fact of the matter is although folly certainly forms a part of life in Oldrents's world, it is a much more compassionate, humanly responsible world than that of the beggars.

The deliberate undercutting of generic expectancy casts a sombre mood over romance in *A Jovial Crew* and shifts it away from the usual moral reassessments found in green world comedy. Thus the total comic effect is akin to that of *The Antipodes* although the dramatic process is different. The two worlds of *A Jovial Crew* do not occupy opposite sides of the moral globe, but when man chooses to live a life antipodal to accepted social and moral existence, he is, as it were, sole-to-sole with those of established custom and human responsibility. Then we have the question, "How can both be found standing upright?" There is something of the "strong moral polarity" in *A Jovial Crew* which Ian Donaldson sees as integral to Jonson's thought. The dichotomy is not, however, as severe as that envisioned by Jonson in *Discoveries*.

How many have I known, [said the learned poet] that would not have their vices hid? Nay, and to be noted, live like *Antipodes* to others in the same City; never see the Sun rise, or set, in so many years; but be as they were watching a Corpse by Torchlight; would not sin the common way; but held that a kind of *Rusticity;* they would do it new, or contrary, for the infamy? They were ambitious of living backward; and at last arrived at that, as they would love nothing but the vices; not vicious customs. It was impossible to reform these natures; they were dried, and hardened in their ill.[35]

Brome was much more conservative and conciliatory than his master. There is, nonetheless, a distinctly Saturnalian quality to Brome's beggar world, an antimasque license which is only dispelled through the enactment of a play-within-a-play concluding the performance. By this time, however, the play has moved from the somber world of moral opposites. In what might seem a rather unsatisfactory contrivance, the harsh beggar world is replaced by a theatrical one.

Old.   But is there a *Play* to be expected and acted by *Beggars?*
Cla.   That is to say, by *Vagabonds;* that is to say by *strolling Players.* They are upon their Purgation. If they can present any thing to please you, they may escape the Law; that is *(a hay)* If not, tomorrow, Gentlemen, shall be acted, *Abuses stripped and whipped* among 'em.
                                                                    (N 3ᵛ; V,i)

The real beggars disappear and the conclusion of the play involves the rehabilitation of player-beggars. Previous economic injustices are reformed; parents and children, ladies and lovers are reconciled; Oldrents discovers Springlove is a lost son; and so the conventional romantic ending appears to be tacked on to what is an anti-romance. Oldrents's final claim, "Here are no *Beggars* . . . no *Rogues,* nor *Players:* But a select Company, to fill this House with Mirth" (O 3ᵛ; V,i), is a prognosis for the future and not a reflection on the past. The prologue warned that the title *A Jovial Crew* may *seem* to promise mirth, but the play itself does not fulfill that promise. It presents a world of displaced characters invaded by others who would desire the same displacement. Player-beggars are joined by would-be players, and both try to act out life rather than live it. Real human harmony remains but a wistful longing, and only briefly can actors in a theater fill a house with mirth. Again as in *The Antipodes,* Brome has turned his art upon itself. In *The Antipodes* he turned play within play within play to satiric purpose, using comedy to serve as its own catharsis; in *A Jovial Crew* he turns romance upon itself, again using character-players to act out their own antiromance. Life itself remains morally open-ended and true human reality is both heart-warming and bone-chilling. Yet the net result is not despair over the inability to achieve harmony outside of the theater. Long-lost Springlove, a symbolic character quite unique in Bromean drama, prognosticates a human impulse which negates despair. In a Caroline world, a far cry from the moral world which Brome envisioned, Springlove characterizes a wistfully hopeful rather than a desperate prognosis.

That satire in the usual Jonsonian sense is not the form of *A Jovial Crew* does not mean that Brome's favorite targets are ignored. When Hearty is encouraging Oldrents to ignore fortunetelling, for example, he gives a series of instances of their equivocations, each directed at objects of Bromean ridicule in other plays. One fortuneteller, says Hearty,

> . . . told a Gentleman
> His son should be a man-killer, and hanged for it;
> Who, after proved a great and rich Physician,
> And with great Fame in the University
> Hanged up in Picture for a grave example.

Such a dig at doctors is worthy of Jonson. Another is the "squint-eyed boy" who was forecast to be a pick-purse and a thief that grew up to be a cunning lawyer. Or, Hearty goes on,

> Was not a Shepherd-boy foretold to be
> A Drunkard, and to get his living from
> Bawds, Whores, Thieves, Quarrellers, and the like?
> And did not he become a Suburb *Justice?*
> And live in Wine and Worship by the Fees
> Racked out of such delinquents?
>
> (B 1ᵛ–B 2ʳ; I,i)

Later, among the beggar band, Brome singles out individuals whose circumstances afford satiric jibes at contemporary London conditions. The poet, who learned his art well in his profession, now practices it better by begging. The courtier, on the other hand, begs for pleasure as his father did before him, "refusing great and constant means from able friends to make him a staid man." After all, *"What's a gentleman but's pleasure"* (C 4ʳ⁻ᵛ; I,i). Justice Clack, who doesn't enter the play until Act V, is at once humorous and the object of satire in his insistence upon punishing before examining, to make the law "surer" on his side (M 3ᵛ; V,i). However, such jibes are only incidental; although incorporating something of Jonson's satiric vision, the play stops short of satire itself and remains contemplative. In its totality of dramatic impression, *The Jovial Crew* stands apart from the mainstream of Caroline comedy, satiric or otherwise. Its distinctive quality, like that of *The Antipodes*, owes its success to Brome's skill in turning conventionality into originality.

CHAPTER 8

Criticism and Revaluation

SIGNIFICANT critical comment on specific Brome plays has been included as each has been discussed. It remains now to survey general critical attitudes taken during the late nineteenth and twentieth centuries and to consider the justice of the positions various critics have taken toward Brome's dramaturgy, his technical strengths and weaknesses, and his contributions to his chosen art form. Perhaps only then can a true value judgment be made.

Much of the criticism has been influenced by a predetermination of Brome's historical position or by a preestablished concept of what morality is, often reflecting the age of the critic rather than that of the playwright. The result is a series of judgments often totally antipathetic to each other. In 1874, J. A. Symonds said, "His [Brome's] view of the world is that of a groom, rather than a gentleman; and the scenes and characters which he depicts are drawn from the experiences of a flunky." He continues, "All the gross and seamy side of human life is shown to us with prosaic ruthlessness."[1] About forty years later, Herbert F. Allen designates Brome's comedies as "Representative of Dramatic Decadence."[2] Using his own definition of decadence, Allen views Brome's handling of sex with Victorian outrage. Another premodern, Clarence Edward Andrews, makes a rather disorganized attempt at Brome's sources and contemporary influences, then concludes that "Brome's work is a mere mosaic of filchings from his predecessors."[3] Writing in 1913, Andrews cites on the fly-leaf of his monograph a quotation from Symonds's review of the 1873 edition of Brome's plays:

The cock in the fable scratched up a pearl from the dunghill, [says Symonds] and it is possible that some ingenious student may discover pearls in what is certainly the rubbish heap of Brome's plays.[4]

That Andrews has chosen to honor this kind of disparagement indicates how little criticism had changed in the years which separated them. On the other hand, Charles M. Gayley, writing about the same time as Allen and Andrews, presented a sound and discerning academic position. Professor Gayley saw Brome as "a product of conscious study of the printed drama, as well as of the power that comes from careful observation of contemporary life and the conditions of the stage." He continues,

On the one hand, he is a recipient: in romantic comedy, a disciple of Shakespeare, Fletcher and Massinger; in the comedy of manners, a follower not merely of Jonson's technique and his theory of humours, but of Dekker's idealism and pathos no less than of his genial portraiture of life. On the other hand, he is a transmitter, even an originator.[5]

Kathleen Lynch, also writing early in this century, was concerned with Brome's influence in the Restoration and her position is equally defensible. "The period of the reign of Charles I," she says, "boasts no great names, by right of peculiar possession, on the honor-roll of its dramatists. Shirley and Brome were Elizabethan survivals. Suckling, with all his talent, wrote eccentric and wayward plays. D'Avenant was unsuited to the work assigned him."[6] This general assessment later leads her to state that "all that is best in the Restoration continuance of Elizabethan dramatic conventions may be illustrated in Congreve's plays," after which she proceeds to show how Richard Brome was one of the strongest of these Elizabethan influences on Congreve.[7] Finally, in 1929, Ashley Thorndike, though somewhat qualified in his appreciation of Brome's art, presented this compromise view:

Brome's plays bring us even closer than those of most of his contemporaries to the Restoration. Their grossness and noisiness, their loose women and tricky spendthrifts, their humours and intrigues remind us of the comedies that were to come in the reign of Charles II. Nevertheless he is still unmistakably of the Elizabethan tradition. He imitates Jonson and Fletcher and Shakespeare. He is not poetical but he tries to be. Though very vulgar he does not dare to be immoral. He delights in human nature, the joy in reporting one's observations on the human species. Though he is imitative and theatrical rather than inventive and imaginative, still does he present a broad and varied view of his Englishmen. The spirit of the great Elizabethans was by no means dead in a theater that could produce "The Antipodes" and "The Merry Beggars."[8]

Professor R. J. Kaufmann, who has written the only recent full-length published study of Brome, places his emphasis upon a "central phase of an historical evolutionary process." As his title indicates, in *Richard Brome, Caroline Dramatist*, Kaufmann insists Brome is distinctively representative of his age and "that the power Brome has as an artist derives from a close and critical relationship to the particular historical and theatrical era in which he wrote."[9] Douglas Sedge agrees with Kaufmann; in his unpublished work, he links Brome's name with that of James Shirley as did Kathleen Lynch but, unlike her, sees them as representative Carolines. He says, "(1) they are, with the exception of Ford, who remains a very special case, the two best dramatists of their day; (2) neither of them fit the conventional notion of the cavalier dramatist who is whole-heartedly a court apologist; (3) they seem. . .to represent the sympathies of distinguishably different areas of the Caroline audience."[10] Both Kaufmann and Sedge consider it necessary to relate Brome to his age, dramatic and historical, and to place him in front of his specific audience before dealing with the moral themes and attitudes or their expression in the plays themselves.

These appraisals indicate some of the attempts to categorize Brome as Elizabethan remnant, Caroline expositor, Restoration precursor, or some combination of all three. Where in this maze does the truth lie? Perhaps the best way to approach the corpus of Brome's plays as representatives of the comic art form is to accept Clifford Leech's hypothesis. Leech says, "A dramatist cannot work without some consideration, even if scornful, of his audience, and his 'tone' will arise from his attitude to their expectations. In trying to reach a correct understanding, therefore, of the drama of any period, we must try first to appreciate the character of its audience: only by knowing that so well that we can discount it shall we be able to follow the playwright's meaning unchecked by oddity of tone."[11] Critics like Leech and later Kaufmann and Sedge have done this groundwork for us admirably. It remains now "to follow the playwright's meaning" unchecked by any "oddity of tone" which might have struck us as alien or discordant. To assess the plays of

Richard Brome with critical fairness, we must first know and accept the milieu in which he wrote; then the subjects and themes which found his drama their most comfortable impulse can be realized and the artistic skill assessed.

We must also recognize that Brome did not live in an artistic vacuum isolated from English dramatic tradition, nor did he spring fully armed from the head of Ben Jonson. He is part of the English comic tradition that had its roots in the interludes, its stage debut in *Gammer Gurton's Needle*, and its self-realization in the character of Falstaff. Indeed, if we could choose but one progenitor for Bromean comic gusto it was the fat knight as much if not more than any of the figures that peopled Jonson's stage. In terms of comic approach and for satiric technique, there is no doubt that Brome was in Jonson's debt, but for consistent morality, for individuality in comic characterization, and for overall dramatic view, he stood in debt to the whole body of English dramatic literature.

On occasion Brome could write badly. Little can be said to redeem *The Queen's Exchange* except, perhaps, its rather ingenious characterization. We can also generalize and say that Brome was no poet. When he attempted philosophical or descriptive verse as opposed to the conversational, he was often careless and unsubtle. His lines frequently lack rhythm and there are an overabundance of long lines containing too many unstressed syllables. He has trouble with the dialogue of serious characters and their lines are often untrue, and somewhat stilted. On occasion, strength of sentiment or internal conflict will save passages of serious poetry but more often meaning is clouded by inadequacy of expression. On the other hand, few could equal his skill in comic repartee. His humor, bawdy or otherwise, found its most successful expression in quick, witty 'retorts' or in longer passages piling one nonsense upon another. Consider one play, *The Sparagus Garden,* and the swift exchange in which Walter and Gilbert compare Samuel to his father, Touchwood:

Walt. . . .Here comes his son, a gentleman of so sweet a disposition, and so contrary to his crab-bed Sire, that a man who never heard of his mother's virtue might wonder who got him for him.
Gil. Not at all I assure you, *Sam* is the father's known son: for the old man you see, is gentle enough, till he be incensed; and the son being moved is as fiery as the father.

Walt. But he is very seldom and slowly moved; his father often and o'
the sudden.
Gil. I prithee would'st thou have green wood take fire as soon as that
which is old and sere?

(B 2ᵛ; I,ii)

Or Tim Hoyden recites ridiculous "Rules and Rudiments" for
being a gentleman:

Principles to be imprinted in the heart of every new made gentleman:
To commend none but himself; to like no man's wit but his own: to
slight that which he understands not: to lend money, & never look for it
again: to take up upon obligation, & lend out upon affectation: to owe
much, but pay little: to sell land, but buy none: to pawn, but never to
redeem again: to fight for a whore: to cherish a Bawd: and defy a
tradesman.

(I 3ʳ⁻ᵛ; IV,ix)

In the same play we also find Brome's delight in verbal devices
such as the extended cliché. In defense of the power of poetry
Samuel intones, "Twas not Achilles' sword, but Homer's pen,
That made brave Hector die the best of men" (The pen is
mightier than the sword). To this solemnity Gilbert quips, "Well
said Poet, thou tumblest out odd ends as well as the best of them"
(F 3ᵛ; III,v). Another favorite was the use of dialect and foreign
accent: Somersetshire *(The Sparagus Garden)*, Yorkshire *(The
Northern Lass)*, and Lancashire *(The Late Lancashire Witches)*,
as well as Dutch *(The Novella)*, French *(The Damoiselle)*, and, of
course, beggars' cant in *The Jovial Crew.*
   The language of love did not come easily to Brome's pen;
scenes of romantic declaration, fortunately few, are awkward
and stagey. He was more skillful in plotting love intrigues than in
supplying lovers with lines to express their feelings. Usually the
joining of lovers takes place early in the last act and either is very
brief or is reported from offstage. When mocking love language,
however, he contrived an exaggerated verbosity characteristic
of his penchant for parody. Apart from the symbolic significance
of the scene, when Quicksands is painting Millicent for her role
as the blackamoor, the ridiculousness of the aged lover is
underscored by his use of outdated Petrarchan metaphor:

Now red and white those two united houses,

> Whence beauty takes her fair name and descent,
> Like peaceful Sisters under one Roof dwelling
> For a small time; farewell. Oh let me kiss ye
> Before I part with you—Now Jewels up
> Into your Ebon Casket. And those eyes,
> Those sparkling eyes, that send forth modest anger
> To singe the hand of so unkind a Painter,
> And make me pull't away and spoil my work,
> They will look straight like Diamonds, set in lead,
> That yet retain their virtue and their value.
>
> (C 5ᵛ; III,i)

The lines are designed to mock Quicksands, the language of love poetry, and a lover's death lament at one blow. In fact, some critics have been quick to accuse Brome of "borrowing" from his betters when the mimicry is fully intended and part of the comic impact. It is true that many attempts at genuine lyricism fall short of their mark and act as intrusions upon the dramatic action; but for the mock-lyric, for the realistic, albeit bawdy ditty, and for songs such as those provided by Springlove and the beggars in *A Jovial Crew* and others which support the major dramatic concerns and distinctions of character in their plays, he deserves nothing but praise.

Richard Brome's greatest strengths as a dramatic artist lay in his plotting and characterization, and he had a positive talent for creating straightforward, broad situation comedy. It would be difficult to find a match for the ease with which he handled two, three, or even four plot lines at once for which he consistently provided intercommunication without relying upon obscure subtleties. Of particular note is his method of establishing motives for the various narrative threads in the first act and of relating particular characters to particular types of intrigues. His most common plot lines seek three somewhat overlapping levels: seriocomic, in which romantic involvements are often found; comic-satirical, peopled by manipulators, impostors, and fools; and the farcical satire of fops, usurers, wenchers, cuckolding wives, and the like. By the end of the first act, the reader is aware not only that it is just a matter of time before the various narrative purposes and cross-purposes will collide and then unite into an hilarious conglomerate ending, but which plot level is the dominant one. From that dominance emerges the "tone" of the play. In other words, we are aware early in a Brome comedy how serious, how amusingly light, how chiding, how biting, or any variation in between, will be the total dramatic impression. As a general rule, the more romantic the play the closer it is to the seriocomic side of the spectrum. In *The Northern Lass,* the romantic attachment between the Lass and Phillip is the most serious, between Fitchow and Tridewell the more comic, and between Holdup and Widgine the parody of love, the farce; any sharp satirical jibes are incidental to the tri-leveling structure here. On the other hand, a play like *A Mad Couple Well Match't* in which there is no young love interest is closer to pure satire; the Bellamy family form a somewhat seriocomic plane, but the main narrative issues involve the Threadwells, who are held up to mocking ridicule, and the Salewares, Careless, and Mrs. Crostill, whose whole moral framework, or lack of it, is exposed.

On occasion, the tri-level structure hinges upon a single touchstone character who is integral to each narrative plane, one character whose relationships to each plot designates these three comic modes. In *The English Moor,* the touchstone is Millicent herself. Her romantic relationship with Theophilus constitutes the seriocomic level, that with her uncle and old Quicksands, the comic-satirical, and that with Nathaniel and the other gallants, the comic-farcical. In *The Damoiselle,* Sir Humphrey Drygrounds provides the comic fulcrum. A father himself, he interacts with three other father figures, each on a different comic level: Brookall, Vermine, and Justice Bumpsey, whose very names support this tri-level structuring. Although not quite so obviously, Cockbrain, the weeder of Covent Garden, has a similar function as a kind of representative of the garden itself. Coming in contact with him and with the garden are the young ladies and gentlemen and their love concerns, the two self-servers, Rooksbill and Crossewill, and then the Citizen, Parson, Tailor, Shoemaker, and Vintner group with their ridiculous pretensions.

Another Bromean plot device should be mentioned—parody. Some examples have already been discussed, such as *The Love-sick Court* as a mock tragicomedy, the main plot of *The Sparagus Garden* as a comic imitation of *Romeo and Juliet,* and the Rafe-Hannah marital agreement as a travesty of the courtly love ethic. A more sophisticated version of parody is achieved through plot inversion. Brome structures *The City Wit,* upon a reversal of the familiar coney-catching plot pattern of which *The Alchemist* can be considered a model. In the Jonson play, Subtle, the arch coney-catcher, is a figure whose humor is greed but who dons the guise of benevolence and apparent generosity toward his various gulls, and then through his intrigues loses all. Crasie, on the other hand, had been a humors figure in his excessive and thoughtless generosity but he now adopts the guise of coney-catcher and through his intrigues gains all.

Eric Bentley has recently pointed out that "plot has not for a long time now been something the reviewers praise a playwright for. They praise him for the characters he has created, and they praise him because they are Real Human Beings. An alternate expression is Believable Human Beings, and the opposite of this is a Type. A Type is a Bad Thing."[12] Unfortunately, a similar attitude toward plotting has been taken by modern literary critics of Renaissance comedy. With the possible exception of romantic comedy, for which Theme seems to be the password, their bent has been to approach comic drama through character at the expense of action. This approach is untenable when we come to characterization in the plays of Richard Brome, because character and action are inextricably joined. Such a variety of plots and interconnecting narrative interests as are found in Brome's comedies provide the arena within which a vast array of stock types, of humors figures, and, on occasion, even characters of fine human verisimilitude take the stage.

Let us consider *The City Wit* again. The central and controlling plot moves because the main character has been foolish and is now wise. Once it is moving, the other characters can take their places because Crasie has provided them a vehicle for action. Some of these figures are stock types: Sarpego, the pedant; Linscy Wolsey, the miser; Jeremy, the wily servant; and, of course, those whom Crasie lists, "the Fool Citizen, the Ass Citizen [and] the Cuckold Citizen" (G 1ᵛ; V,i). Pyannet Sneakup, the magpie, is a fine humors figure and the surprise plotted for her at the end of the play is superbly fitting: what better comeuppance for a woman who has insisted on wearing the pants in the family than to find out that the wealthy widow to whom she has married off her nitwit son actually does wear breeches?[13] The complex Crasie is separate from both the stock and the humors characterization. He is enlightened, with an understanding of human motivation that simultaneously makes him Brome's mouthpiece and the norm for human behavior. The very fact

that Crasie has changed and is willing to act against rather than
condone excess and irresimilitude gives him a verisimilitude the
other characters are not allowed. The action begins with his
awareness and determination:

> Is this the end of unsuspicious Freeness?
> Are open hands of Cheerful Piety
> A helpful bounty, and most easy Goodness,
> Rewarded thus?
> Is, to be honest, termed to be a fool?
> Respect it Heaven. Bear up still merry heart.
> Droop not: But scorn the world's unjust despising.
> *Who through Goodness sinks, his fall's his Rising.*
>
> (B 3ʳ; I,ii)

and ends with Crasie being his own example of the principles of
honesty and generosity:

> Think of no losses. Sirs, you shall have none;
> My honest case being but to keep mine own.
> What, by my slights, I got more than my due,
> I timely will restore again to you.
>
> (G 3ᵛ; V,i)

Thus character instigates plot and plot proves character.

Looking at characterization in Brome's comedies as a whole,
we can group some who are true stock types out of Roman and
Italianate comedy. Wily servants abound; Pantaloni, the aged
lover, and Guardagni, the miser, neatly pair off in *The Novella;* in
The Northern Lass are found Captain Anvile, the braggart
soldier, Vexham, the dishonest lawman, and Widgine, the
simpleton lover; that the Wits and Dainty in *The Court Begger*
have specific contemporary identification does not change them
from being stock, self-serving fops, and in fact it enhances their
value as objects of laughter. Usurers can be as dangerous as
Vermine in *The Damoiselle* or as easy to outwit as Quicksands in
The English Moor, and ambitious villains as high-born as
Stratocles in *The Love-sick Court* or as low-born as his servant,
Matho. In fact, it is often part of Brome's plot-character amalgam
to provide narrative intrigues to expose exactly the same
character type at various levels of London's class-structured

society, the point being that these stock figures can be found and ridiculed in any social stratum.

A clear distinction must be made between these stock types and the humors figure. Asper, in the Induction to Jonson's *Every Man Out of His Humour,* says humor can be defined

> As when some one peculiar quality
> Doth so possess a man, that it doth draw
> All his affects, his spirits, and his powers,
> In their confluctions, all to run one way,
> This may be truly said to be a Humour.[14]

This sense of a man "possess[ed]" is what should separate the humors figure from the stock type. The stock character is an abstract form fashioned in concrete, of specific and relatively unchanging proportion. The humors figure, on the other hand, is one which has at base a variable human temperament but has become preoccupied and impelled by some whim, some idiosyncratic mode of behavior, some obsessive desire. The audience accepts the stock type for what he is and does not concern itself with psychological motivation for his actions. With the humors figure the audience *is* interested in what makes him act in this way or that.

Covent-Garden Weeded presents a group of characters which illustrate Richard Brome's use of the humors concept both directly and indirectly. Crossewill is typical of a man "possess[ed]"; his "effects, his spirits, and his powers" all run to inordinate self-will. His name indicates his contrariness is an obsession to cross the will of anyone else, particularly that of his own children. By presenting Crossewill as a humors figure Brome succeeds, as Professor Sedge has pointed out, in reducing the whole "concept of excessive parental authority to absurdity."[15] Ironically, Crossewill's explanation of his daughter's supposed insistence actually reveals the basis of his own.

But she has a humour. . .to make me a match-broker, her marriage-Maker; when I tell you friend, there have been so many untoward matches of Parents' making, that I have sworn she shall make her own choice, though it be of one I hate. Make me her match-maker! Must I obey her, or she me, ha?

(B 3ᵛ; I,i)

To make her own choice is exactly what Katherine wants. She, like her brothers, Mihil and Gabriel, adopt a humor to thwart a humor and thus we have the Jonsonian concept being brought into play both directly and by that comic inversion of which Brome is so fond.

The Court Begger has two main humors characters. Mendicant is possessed by the idea that he can raise his state by court suits which he trusts to mediators among the royal favorites. Throughout the play, however, we are aware of the Mendicant underneath this willful and ridiculous pursuit and are not surprised when he is purged of his humor at the end of the play. The second direct humors figure is Lady Strangelove. Her obsession is to be wooed and when she has won men's affection to cast them off. Sir Raphael warns her:

I speak to only you; to conjure (if you can) that spirit of scorn out of you; which you have taken in, and long affected for a humor, til it is grown so familiar, so inherent in you, that you have won the title of the humorous Lady by it; and drawn a scorn upon yourself.

(O 7^r; II,i)

Her purgation comes through a double humors figure, Sir Ferdinand, who, already taken with vaingloriousness, adopts or feigns still another humor, that of love-madness for Lady Strangelove. When, under the guise of insanity he attempts to seduce her, the lady is shocked out of her proclivity for playing games with others' emotions. When he in turn is caught by an ingenious trick, he abandons both the real and the adopted humor and joins with the others to bring Mendicant to his senses. Thus again, we have Brome using the humors concept in two different ways in the same play.

A Jovial Crew cannot be left out in any summary of Brome's skill in characterization. The kind of comic inversion achieved through plot reversals has been discussed earlier, and this generic sophistication provides many opportunities for variety in characterization. The stock types, though in minor roles, are well represented in Clack, the confused Justice, and in the performing beggars: impoverished Poet, knavish Attorney, cowardly Soldier, and cunning Prophet. Then there are three kinds of humors figures. The simplest of these are the two young gentlemen, Vincent and Hilliard. Obsessed with satisfying their ladies' slightest whims, one night of beggary is enough to shock them back to a sense of reality. Meriel and Rachael, on the other hand, not only feel the usual youthful rebellion against their father's "Rule and Government," but his melancholy has produced a fixation on its opposite. "We must out of the house," is their cry. "We cannot live but by laughing, and that aloud, and nobody sad within hearing." Their return to a sense of perspective takes longer for they are headstrong and simply refuse to admit that their compulsion for freedom has imposed greater restrictions than they had anticipated. The complexity of Oldrents as a humors figure lies in his determination to take on a persuasion opposite to his "disposition to sadness"—*he will be jovial* and he deliberately adopts this antihumor not because he has any particular end in view but merely because he wills it into being. Only when the play-within-the-play puts all the narrative complications into perspective and the masque-antimasque parodies the humor-antihumor does Oldrents regain his usual admirable stability.

On the surface, Springlove may also appear as a humors figure. In spite of his love and respect for Oldrents, he does feel the compulsion each vernal season to cast off his responsibilities and become a vagabond. This impulse, however, is not a humor; it is a genuine part of Springlove's nature and is given a logical explanation in the quality of his birth. Born of a gypsy mother and the "ancient Esquire," Oldrents, Springlove has a duality of makeup which conditions dual responses. He never acts *other than* his genuine nature would dictate, bifurcated though it may be, and thus achieves a human verisimilitude denied to stock types and only hinted at in humors figures. Springlove's human verisimilitude is strengthened by his internal conflict, and the resolution of this conflict is the thematic resolution of the whole play: true freedom does not exist divorced from all social obligation, and in virtuous service is freedom.

Another character of genuine nature is Justice Bumpsey in *The Damoiselle*. At once concerned for his daughter's welfare in a marriage to impoverished gentry and impressed by the young groom's gravity and independence, Bumpsey conceives of a plan which illustrates both of his natural inclinations—generosity and thrift. With Drygrounds representing wasted means and Ver-mine greed for gain to flank him, Bumpsey represents no excess at all, but, rather, good sense and good husbandry. It is true that he has mannerisms which we find funny but it is his manner we laugh at, not his person or his values.

Perhaps because satire and farce, the comic impulses which are most characteristic of Bromean comedy, do not provide ready vehicles for them, characters having deep-rooted human verisimilitude are relatively infrequent in Brome's plays. Even with his skill in handling feminine roles (far superior to Jonson's), Brome usually skirts fully developed internal conflict. Although he depicts his whores, his neglected wives, his shrews, with the fine line of caricature, only his innocent heroines move beyond stock types or humors figures and achieve a kind of humanity which most of Jonson's figures lack. They come to represent a youthful determination to action, based not upon whim or mere will to be perverse but upon an insistence of self-identity which is at one with a natural life force. It is in this way, rather than through inner conflict, that they achieve a kind of archetypal universality, different though it may be from that of a Springlove or, to a lesser degree, a Justice Bumpsey.

Finally, we must credit Brome for the fine theatricality of his plays, a quality too often ignored by literary critics. Swiftness of movement and diversity in comic pacing are characteristic of most of his works. When Brome is at his best, the stage is almost invariably alive with action, and for the reader an inward "theater" eye is needed for full appreciation. He appears to have conceived plot first and then peopled his action with appropriate characters, and in this way he is like Shakespeare. We never have the impression, as is sometimes the case with Jonson, that Brome first thought about what he wanted to satirize and then looked about for a vehicle for his attack. His morality or his thematic concerns are implicit rather than explicit. As a result, in all but a few of his plays, the plots move with surety and the characters move with realistic action and reaction. Brome's dramas are *at home* on the stage. Although they may be notable for an absence of an obviously asserted didacticism, their moral convictions are strong and their representation of Renaissance life is pungent. In the way that Sidney used the word, they *delight* both mind and eye. Or, as their author speaks for them:

All we pretend is but Mirth and Sense.[16]

Notes and References

Chapter One

1. In the 1652 dedication to *The Jovial Crew*, the playwright refers to the comedy as "this issue of my Old age" (sig. A 2ʳ) and in 1653 Alexander Brome says in the epistle prefatory to the first *Five New Plays* that the poet is dead. All quotations from Brome's plays are from first editions unless otherwise stated.

2. C. H. Herford, Percy and Evelyn Simpson, eds. *Ben Jonson*, 11 vols. (Oxford, 1925–51), VI (1938), 13. All further references to Jonson are from this edition unless otherwise stated.

3. Gerald Eades Bentley, *The Jacobean and Caroline Stage*, 7 vols. (Oxford, 1941–68), III (1956), 49–50. Hereafter cited as Bentley. If, in a commendatory poem written for Thomas Randolph on the publication of his *Poetical Varieties* in 1637, Brome's welcome to the young poet, "Now (most happily) when Poets old are sinking too!" (sig. A 4ᵛ), is a jocular reference to Brome's own advancing years, then a date somewhat earlier than 1590 may be likely.

4. Alwin Thayer, "Was Richard Brome an Actor?" *MLN* XXXVI (1921), 89.

5. Professor Thayer presents the item as it had been reprinted by C. C. Stopes in "Shakespeare's Fellows and Followers" *(Shakespeare Jahrbuck* XLVI [1910], 94), in which Mrs. Stopes misread a number of the names. As it is printed in "Dramatic Records: The Lord Chamberlain's Office" (Allardyce Nicoll and Eleanore Boswell, *Malone Society Collections* II, 3 [1931], 347. Hereafter cited as M.S.C.), the warrant reads:

A Warrant to swear the Queen of Bohemia's Players Grooms of his Maᵗᵉˢ Chambers in ordinary without fee. vizt) Joseph Moore, Alexander Foster, Robert Gylman, Richard Broom. John Lillie, [Richard Wickes] Wm. Rogers, George Lillie, Abel Swinarton, George Giles [John Jewell], Oliver Jones.

It is also worth noting that both Joseph More and Alexander Foster were appearing in the provinces with this company as early as 1611–12.

6. *Works,* IV, 119–20.

7. Joseph Quincy Adams, *The Dramatic Records of Sir Henry Herbert* (New Haven, 1917), p. 26. "There is nothing in Herbert's entry

149

to indicate 'Young Johnson' was the son of Ben" (Bentley, III, 69).

8. Bentley, III, 81.

9. In addition to the "good applause" which the author says was accorded the play "in former times," Crasie, the city wit who speaks the Prologue added in the revision, says that there will be some in the theater who have seen and heard the play before he "that bear the title, wore a Beard" (sig. A 2^v).

10. Bentley, II, 389–90.

11. Ann Haaker in "The Plague, the Theatre, and the Poet" (*Renaissance Drama*, n.s. I [1968], 283–306), gives a full discussion of the court proceedings and the contracts which led up to them. Another possible reference to his hardships during the plague may occur in Brome's commendatory poem to Thomas Nabbes's masque *Microcosmus*, published in 1637. In it Brome wishes that the restraints be taken off the theaters "in part for mine own sake as well as thine" (sig. A 4^r).

12. Sig. a 2^v–3^r.

13. Edmond Malone, "Shakespeare, Ford, and Jonson," *The Plays and Poems of William Shakespeare* (London, 1790). J. Q. Adams (op. cit., 9–13) discusses the lost Herbert office-book from which Malone was working.

14. George Bremner Tennant, ed., *The New Inn, Yale Studies in English* XXXIV (1908), xxii–xxxiii.

15. George Thorn-Drury, ed., *The Poems of Thomas Randolph* (London, 1929), p. 83.

16. Sig. A 3^r.

17. M.S.C., II, 3, 399; W. W. Greg, ed., *A Bibliography of the English Printed Drama to the Restoration*, 4 vols. (London, 1939–59), 980. Hereafter cited as Greg; *Stationers' Register*, Sept. 9, 1653.

18. Bentley, III, 83–84.

19. Greg, II, 611.

20. When speaking of Jonson's magnetism and the respect with which this man was viewed by his literary contemporaries, Herford and Simpson say, "Its potency was yet more signally shown in the total absence during Jonson's later years, of pronounced and declared reaction from his ways. The clamorous disapproval and derision which greeted some of his later plays did not come from the men who were making literature; they rallied in his defense; or if they gently criticized, it was in the name of the greater things he himself had done before" (*Works*, I, 108).

21. Sig. a 1^r.

22. Sig. A 4^r–B 1^r.

23. Bentley, III, 89–91.

24. M.S.C., II, 3, 410.

25. Professor Haaker (op cit., pp. 296–306) cities both documents in full in her article.

26. Bentley, III, 76.

27. According to Brome's response to the complaint charges, this profit was to come from a day of his choosing within ten days after the play opened (Haaker, op. cit., p. 302).

28. Ralph J. Kaufmann, *Richard Brome: Caroline Dramatist* (New York and London, 1961), p. 18.

29. Bentley, I, 296.

30. Philip Bordinat, "A Study of the Salisbury Court Theatre," Diss., University of Birmingham, 1952, pp. 51–52.

31. Haaker, op. cit., p. 304.

32. Although this play is not extant, its title appears in the *Stationers' Register:*

1640 Mar. 19. Ent. (F.) Constable: lic. Wykes: three plays called, *Sparagus Garden, The Antipodes,* and *Wit in a Madness.* (Greg, II, 975).

As the first two plays mentioned in the *Register* listing definitely belong to the Salisbury Court company, the best guess, as Bentley suggests (III, 72), is that *Wit in a Madness* belongs in the 1635–39 period and that all three plays were turned over to the publisher by the playwright in a fit of rebellious pique after he had broken off his relationship with Salisbury Court even though the terms of the contract prohibited publication without the consent of the company.

33. Haaker, op. cit., p. 304.

34. Brome breaks with his usual practice of avoiding personalities by indulging in devastating ridicule of Davenant in *The Court Begger.*

35. *Lachrymas Musarum* . . . Collected and set forth by R. B. (London, 1649), sig. E 7ᵛ-8ʳ; pp. 74–75.

36. Some commendatory poems which Brome, in turn, contributed to his friends' publications have been mentioned earlier. Others were written for Shakerley Marmion's *Cupid and Psyche* (1637), Humphrey Hill's *A Night's Search* (1640), and John Tatham's *Fancies Theatre* (1640).

37. Sir Richard Baker, *A Chronicle of the Kings of England*, 3rd ed., augmented by Edward Philips (London, 1660), p. 603 (misnumbered 503).

38. M. C. Bradbrook, *Shakespeare the Craftsman* (New York and London, 1969), p. 46.

39. Commendatory verse to *A Jovial Crew* (sig. A 4ʳ).

40. Douglas Sedge, "Social and Ethical Concerns in Caroline

Drama," Diss., University of Birmingham, 1966, p. 330.

41. Ben Jonson, Prologue to *Everyman in His Humour*, *Works*, III, 303.

42. *"To the* Stationer, *on the publishing* Mr. Brome's *Comedies,"* *Five New Plays* (1653), sig. A 4^v (Q misnumbered A 2^v)–A 5^r.

43. Francis Beaumont and John Fletcher, *Comedies and Tragedies* (London, 1647), sig. G 1^r.

44. "The Musical Art of Richard Brome's Comedies," *Renaissance Drama* n.s. VII (1976), 220.

Chapter Two

1. Bentley, III, 82–83. According to Giles Floyd, *The Northern Lass* was last acted in 1738 ("A Critical Edition of Brome's *A Jovial Crew* with Introduction, Textual Notes, and Glossary," Diss., University of Iowa, 1943, p. xxviii).

2. Sig. A 3^v.

3. Sig. A 3^r.

4. Sig. A 4^r.

5. Sig. A 2^v–3^r.

6. Richard Levin, *The Multiple Plot in English Renaissance Drama* (Chicago, 1971), p. 55.

7. Ibid., pp. 55–56.

8. This is an obscene pun on "purse," as it means both wallet and sexual cavity.

9. Q signature misprinted as A 3.

10. Professor Ingram has shown the dramatic significance of the lass's first song. While Constance is singing *"You say my Love is but a Man"* (E 1^{r-v}; II, iii), she is interrupted by Anvile. He is disguised as Sir Philip, but he comes not as a serious suitor as Master Nonsense does later, but as a potential seducer. Professor Ingram says that "it is an unexceptional lyric" and then goes on:

. . .The important thing is that the words are sufficiently vague to suit Constance's frame of mind as aptly as they do the quite contrary one of Anvile. For Constance the song sums up what she has just been saying about Sir Philip: for Anvile, who thinks he is in a bawdy house. . .this is just the kind of enticing song he expects to hear in such a place, He interprets it according to his lewd hopes and calls it "a sweet prologue to the interlude." (op. cit. p. 225).

11. Ingram, op. cit., p. 226.

12. Ingram, loc. cit.

13. Northrop Frye, *The Anatomy of Criticism* (Princeton, 1957), p. 163.

14. Kaufmann, op. cit., p. 180.

15. Robert B. Sharpe, "The Sources of Richard Brome's *The Novella,*" *SP* XXX (1933), 85.
16. Floyd, op. cit., p. xxxiv.
17. OED, *ruffiano*, obs. A protector or confederate of courtesans.
18. Sedge, op. cit., p. 113.
19. Sir Edmund Gosse and T. J. Wise, eds., *The Complete Works of Charles Algernon Swinburne*, 20 vols. (London, 1925-27), XII, 330. Hereafter cited as Swinburne.
20. Professor Sedge (op. cit., p. 209) suggests that "in recounting their pretence they [Meanwell and Rashley] show a mature disdain for all the paraphernalia and procedure of the [dueling] code."
21. Herbert Allen, *A Study of the Comedies of Richard Brome* (Stanford, 1912), p. 47.
22. Jackson I. Cope has noted Brome's debt here to Jonson's *The Masque of Blackness* (*The Theater and the Dream: From Myth to Metaphor in Renaissance Drama* [Baltimore and London, 1973], p. 141).
23. Richard H. Jefferson, "Some Aspects of Richard Brome's Comedies of Manners," Diss., University of Wisconsin, 1955, pp. 146-52. Jackson Cope in dealing with what he sees as the "tragicomic aspects of the plot" also says it "focuses on the aggressively male disguise of Dionisia (loc. cit.).

Chapter Three

1. Arthur Bivens Stonex traces the development of this plot from the early and simple allegory on avarice in his article "The Usurer in Elizabethan Drama" (*PLMA* XXXI [1916], 190-210). *The Damoiselle*, he says, was "one of the last of the usurer plays to appear before the closing of the theatres. . ." (p. 210).
2. Swinburne, p. 201.
3. Floyd, op. cit., p. xxviii.
4. Swinburne, loc. cit.
5. As Bumpsey explains:

> Now mark; if you increase,
> Or keep that half, then, doubtless, I shall do,
> As well with t'other for you: If you diminish
> Or waste it all, I'll do the like with my part.

(B 6ᵛ; I, ii)

6. Kaufmann, op. cit., pp. 131, 139.
7. Ibid., p. 138.
8. OED, *tony*, obs. Cheated, swindled. The OED cites this line as an example of the use of the word.

9. Sedge, op. cit., p. 237.
10. Bentley, III, 59-60. Bentley suggests that the confusion with which the Prologue is printed in the 1653 edition was "perhaps derived from the state of the playhouse manuscript from which it was set up." If the play were, indeed, revised as well as revived, the state of the manuscript might also account for the confusion in the assignment of some speeches.
11. Professor Kaufmann also points out (op. cit., p. 52n) that to underscore this theme "Brome reiterates the words 'honesty' or 'honest' fourteen (14) times in less than two pages of text [sig. A 6^v-7^r; I,i]."
12. OED 25, *composition*. An agreement for the payment (or the payment by agreement) of a sum of money, in lieu of the discharge of some other obligation or in a different way from that required by the original contract; a compounding; *spec.* an agreement by which a creditor accepts a certain proportion of a debt, in satisfaction, from an insolvent debtor.
13. Her name, Pyannet, means chatterer, *magpie*, or, more insidiously, *maggot-pie*. A number of the names in *The City Wit* have meanings beyond what might appear obvious. Crasie, according to the OED, at one time meant impaired, broken down in estate, ruined, bankrupt. Sarpego is a general term for a creeping or spreading disease. Linsey Wolsey, which was originally a cloth mixture, by the Renaissance also meant any *strange medley;* confusion, nonsense.
14. Q Lanthorne-lanthorn-penis.
15. Ronald Bayne, "Lesser Jacobean Dramatists," *CHEL* VI, 229.
16. Kaufmann, op. cit., pp. 151-68.
17. Ibid., p. 152.
18. Sedge, op. cit., p. 252.
19. *Statutes of the Realm*, Printed by Command of His Majesty King George III (London, 1810-28), III (1817), 803.
20. Q Doctor indicated as playing the part of Jupiter is obviously not on stage.
21. Swinburne, p. 331.
22. Felix E. Schelling, *Elizabethan Drama 1558-1642*, 2 vols. (London, 1908), II, 273.

Chapter Four

1. The play is called *The Weeding of Covent-Garden* on the title page; it is equally often referred to by its running title *The Covent-Garden Weeded*.
2. This utilization of a popular locale to establish a kind of unity for comedies of manners and intrigues is discussed by Richard Perkinson in his article "Topographical Comedy in the Seventeenth Century"

(*English Literary History* III [1936], 270–90) and by Theodore Miles in "Place-Realism in a Group of Caroline Plays" (*Review of English Studies* XVIII [1942], 428–40). Other plays discussed in the group are Shakerley Marmion's *Hollands Leaguer* (1613), Thomas Nabbes's *Tottenham Court* (1633), and Thomas Jordan's *The Walks of Islington and Hogsden* (1641). Neither Perkinson nor Miles includes *A Mad Couple Well Match't*.

3. Miles, op. cit., p. 433.

4. Floyd, op. cit., p. xxvii.

5. Kaufmann's comment (op. cit., p. 80) that the description of Gabriel's humor (E 2^{r-v}; III,i) can only be described as a rudimentary psychiatric "case history" makes Gabriel an interesting forerunner for Peregrine Joyless in *The Antipodes*.

6. This refers to the identification of Dainty in *The Court Begger* as Inigo Jones. Sir John Suckling, satirized with Jones and Davenant in *The Court Begger*, comes in for his share of ridicule in a prefatory poem to *The Covent-Garden Weeded* called "Upon *Aglaura* printed in Folio." In the poem Brome says, among other things,

> *This great voluminous Pamphlet may be said*
> *To be like one that hath more hair than head;*
> *More excrement than body. Trees, which sprout*
> *With broad leaves, have still the smallest fruit.* (A 2^{r})

The poem was obviously added to Brome's manuscript later, as *Aglaura* was not written until late 1637 and published in folio form in 1638. Bentley points out that "according to contemporary accounts, Suckling gave the play to the King's Men instead of selling it, like a good work-a-day playwright, and he paid for special costumes and, according to Aubrey, scenery as well. Richard Brome could not forget this unfair competition with the poor professionals and grumbled about it repeatedly" (V, 1206).

7. In 1631, Frances Russell, fourth Earl of Bedford, engaged Inigo Jones "to lay out Covent Garden and to build a church in the piazzas which were projected" (E. Beresford Chancellor, *The Annals of Covent Garden* [London, 1930], p. 33).

8. Jonson, VII, 209–10.

9. OED, *rook*. Applied to persons as an abusive or disparaging term; a cheat, a swindler, or sharper. Thomas Dekker in *The Wonderful Year* (pub. 1603) uses "Rook" to mean a literary thief; "So many Rookes, catchpolls of poesy, That feed upon the fallings of hye wit" (*Works* [1884–86], I, 89).

10. The jibe is based on the professional prestige Inigo Jones enjoyed as an architect. Cockbrain's comment places Jones back in the building trade where Brome obviously thinks he belongs.

11. Kaufmann, op. cit., pp. 75–87. This theme is not the exclusive

prerogative of this play. In *The Queen's Exchange*, written about the same time, Segebert's children take polarized positions in relation to their father. In other plays, attempts to enforce marriage produce the same result. In *The Novella* Victoria takes on the role of a courtesan; Millicent in *The English Moor* is disguised as a blackamoor.

12. Miles, op. cit., pp. 434-35.

13. Kaufmann, op. cit., pp. 59-60.

14. Clarence Edward Andrews, *Richard Brome: A Study of His Life and Work* (New York, 1913), p. 56.

15. Bentley, III, 81. The place of *The New Academy* in Brome's chronology is discussed in Chapter 1.

16. Kaufmann, op cit., pp. 53-57. John Payne Collier *(History of English Dramatic Poetry* II [London, 1831], 22-24) cites evidence that a company of French actors performed in London in 1629 (consult A. H. Upham, *The French Influence in English Literature* [New York, 1908], pp. 321-22). The lack of success of this endeavor, however, renders the occasion unlikely evidence for dating *The New Academy* earlier than Kaufmann suggests.

17. Upham, op. cit., p. 331.

18. The general influence of this new wave of Platonics upon such writers as Suckling and Davenant has been discussed by Jefferson Butler Fletcher ("Precieuses at the Court of Charles I," *Journal of Comparative Literature* I [1903], 120-53); A. H. Upham (op. cit., pp. 308-64); and more recently by C. V. Wedgwood ("Comedy in the Reign of Charles I," *Studies in Social History,* ed. John Harold Plumb [London, 1955], pp. 109-37); and George Sensabaugh ("Love Ethics in Platonic Court Drama 1625-1642," *Huntington Library Quarterly* I [1937-38], 277-304).

19. Fletcher, op. cit., p. 150.

20. Sedge, op. cit., p. 171.

21. Swinburne, p. 336.

22. Ram Alley was a well-known place of sanctuary in London south of Fleet Street where characters of questionable reputation gathered. The location is mentioned in *Return from Parnassus* (1601-1603), I, ii, 274; Massinger's *A New Way to Pay Old Debts* (1621) II, ii, 123; and Jonson's *A Staple of News* (1626) II, v, 113. Its associations for the audience would be immediate. Another point of interest is that a new edition of David, Lord Barrey's play *Ram Alley* (1607-1608; pub. 1611) was printed in 1636, presumably to profit by the popularity of place-realism.

23. Kaufmann, op. cit., p. 56.

24. C. V. Wedgwood (op. cit., pp. 122-23) compares this situation to similar ones occurring earlier in Marston's *Eastward Ho* (1605) and in *The City Madam* (1637) by George Chapman.

25. Sedge, op. cit., p. 174.

26. Schelling, op. cit., pp. 272–73.

27. Floyd, op. cit., p. xxvi.

28. Kaufmann, op. cit., pp. 57, 182.

29. Swinburne, pp. 329–30.

30. Charles E. Guardia, "Richard Brome as a Follower of Ben Jonson," Diss., Louisiana State University, 1939, p. 46.

31. Elizabeth Cook, "The Plays of Richard Brome," *More Books* XXII (1947), 299.

Chapter Five

1. The full analysis of *The Love-sick Court* occurs in Chapter 7.

2. Examples of Brome writing plays catering to the popularity of place-realism are discussed in Chapter 4. *The Late Lancashire Witches*, which took advantage of the public interest in the 1633 witch trials, is discussed in Chapter 7.

3. *The Lover's Melancholy* (1627), *The Broken Heart* (1625–33), *Beauty in a Trance* (lost, 1630), *'Tis Pity She's a Whore* (1629?–33), *Love's Sacrifice* (1632?).

4. Even Anthynus's words to his father are reminiscent of Cordelia's. "Less than due I dare not give you," he responds, "and more were to abuse you" (B 4^r; I,ii).

5. When the Saxon lords suggest Segebert might be executed, Bertha accuses them of cruelty. Neither will she allow his lands and goods to be forfeit.

6. Lawrence Babb, *The Elizabethan Malady* (East Lansing, Mich., 1951), p. 164n.

7. Cope, op. cit., p. 140.

8. OED, *genius*. 1.c. (A person's) *good, evil genius:* The two mutually opposed spirits (in Christian language *angels*) by whom every person was supposed to be attended throughout his life.

9. Cope, loc. cit.

10. Babb, op. cit., p. 153.

11. The idea that divine mercy can restore a distempered mind is ancient. Perhaps there is some connection between fools' curative powers and the belief that they were touched by God. However, Enid Welsford gives a number of examples of actual fools with healing powers (*The Fool* [London, 1935], pp. 129–33), and Lawrence Babb cites diverse medical tracts which suggest diversion and gaiety as cures for mental fixations (op. cit., pp. 39–40). Earlier in the play Jeffrey is sought to do Osriik "more good than a whole College of Physicians" (C 3^v; II,ii).

12. Bayne, op. cit., p. 231.

13. Frye, op. cit., pp. 182–84.

14. It is interesting to note that Philip Massinger in *A Very Woman* (1634), which he revised from an earlier collaboration with John Fletcher (1619–22), retains two supernatural figures, "Genius Bonus" and "Genius Malus." However, *The Queen and Concubine* is the last Renaissance play to include such a presence. The figure does not appear in Brome's source.

15. It is this quality in Eulalia of being an allegorical constant which R. J. Kaufmann has failed to realize when he says, "Eulalia is equivalent to Prospero" (op. cit., p. 103). There are certain narrative parallels between *The Queen and Concubine* and *The Tempest*, but Eulalia is not Prospero. Shakespeare's exiled Duke himself provided the narrative circumstances within which his brother could depose him; Prospero is desirous of revenge; his magic comes from books, not Divine Providence; he must be instructed by Ariel in order to turn from self-satisfaction to a love of common good. There is no turn or change in Eulalia; she is an allegorical touchstone by which all other characters can be measured. Perhaps the closest Shakespearean character she comes to is Cordelia. Eulalia's story might be seen as what happened to Cordelia after her banishment; after she was the victim of infected reason but held her own reason inviolate and, therefore, could assume a prelapsarian state.

16. Ashley H. Thorndyke, *English Comedy* (New York, 1929), pp. 247–48.

17. Emil Koeppel, "Brome's *Queen and Concubine*," *Quellen und Forschungen* LXXXII (Strassburg, 1897), 209–18.

18. Alexander B. Grossart, ed., *Works of Robert Greene* (London, 1881–86), V, 191. All further quotations from *Penelope's Web* are from this edition.

19. Professor Sedge (op. cit., pp. 267–68) suggests that Brome is presenting "the corrupting effect of society in conditioning young people into an implicit acceptance of the social climbing ethic." In view of Brome's attacks on social climbers in other plays, this is no doubt true.

20. William Shakespeare, *As You Like It, The Riverside Shakespeare*, ed. G. Blakemore Evans (Boston, 1974), V, iv, 167–68.

21. Greene, V, 168.

22. Greene, V, 181.

23. Greene, V, 187.

24. Greene, V, 193.

25. Q signature misprinted as C 3.

26. Greene, V, 179.

27. Schelling, op. cit., p. 337.

28. Kaufmann, op. cit., p. 92.

Chapter Six

1. Bentley, III, 69.
2. Joseph Quincy Adams, "Hill's List of Early Plays in Manuscript," *Library* 4th Ser. XX (1939), 73.
3. Bentley, III, 59.
4. Greg, II, 993.
5. Bentley, III, 76.
6. Robert Martin Grant, "Is *The Late Lancashire Witches* a Revision?" *Modern Philology* XIII (1915), 253-65.
7. Wallace Notestein, *A History of Witchcraft in England 1558-1718*, American Historical Association (Washington, D.C., 1911), pp. 146-60.
8. Martin, op. cit., p. 255.
9. Arthur Melville Clark, *Thomas Heywood: Playwright and Miscellanist* (Oxford, 1931), pp. 121-27.
10. Ibid., pp. 120-21.
11. Thomas Heywood and Richard Brome, *The Late Lancashire Witches*, Printed by Thomas Harper for Benjamin Fisher (London, 1634), sig. B 1ᵛ. Subsequent citations are from this edition.
12. Clark, op. cit., pp. 242-44.
13. OED, *point*. The lace with which a cod-piece is fastened.
14. OED, *Skimington*. A ludicrous procession, formerly common in villages and country districts, usually intended to bring ridicule or odium upon a woman or her husband in cases where one was unfaithful to, or mistreated, the other. [Or] the man or woman personating the ill-used husband or the offending wife in the procession. . . .
15. OED, *vail*. Doff or take off, esp. out of respect or as a sign of submission.
16. OED, *comrague arch*. [f com + rogue. In the 17th century often jocularly confused with comrade]. A fellow rogue.
17. A. W. Ward, *A History of English Dramatic Literature to the Death of Queen Anne* (London, 1875), II, 122.

Chapter Seven

1. Swinburne, p. 335.
2. Alfred Harbage, *Cavalier Drama* (London, 1936), p. 158.
3. Kaufmann, op. cit., p. 109ff.
4. Sedge, op. cit., p. 209.
5. Cited in Sensabaugh, op. cit., p. 279. The letter is dated June 3, 1634.

6. Kaufmann, op. cit., p. 120.

7. In the tragicomedies the action begins in and then moves out of the court world.

8. As, for example, he does in the Prologue to *The Court Begger.*

9. For specific examples interpolated into the dialogue from *The Voyages and Travels of Sir John Mandeville* and also from Robert Burton's *Anatomy of Melancholy,* consult the explanatory notes in Ann Haaker's edition of *The Antipodes* (Lincoln, Nebraska, 1966).

10. Babb, op. cit., p. 123. Professor Babb also points out that there are no medical resemblances to Hughball's method in medical writing of the period.

11. In Ford's play, Palador, Prince of Cyprus, is in a melancholic condition as a result of his love for the lost Eroclea. His doctor, Corax, reveals the cause of the Prince's lethargy through the "Masque of Melancholy." The masque does not effect a cure, however. The Prince is only restored to health when united to his love. Brome, on the other hand, uses his masque at the end of *The Antipodes* as an illustration of what the plays-within-the-play have already effected.

12. Swinburne, op. cit., pp. 334-35.

13. Professor Bordinat (op. cit., pp. 166-68) indicates scenes in which Letoy, Joyless, and Diana must have been watching from the upper stage. Letoy is with them at first and then descends to the main acting area from which he both directs the action and calls up comments to the viewers above. Later, as the play-within-the-play comes to an end, Letoy invites them down for "their parts are next." Bordinat also gives a good argument (pp. 180-83) that when By-Play tells of Peregrine's mad intrusion into the actors' "Tyring-house," he is describing the storage rooms of the Salisbury Court Theatre. The lines (sig. G 1^v-2^r; III,v), indicate, says Bordinat, that costumes were stored in an upper room and stage properties in a lower, thus facilitating quick movement of set pieces on and off the main acting platforms (i.e., *a table set forth, covered with treasure* [sig. K 3^v; V,iv]).

14. Andrews, op. cit., pp. 122-24.

15. The exposure of the guilt of Claudius in Hamlet's "mousetrap" scene is not the least of these.

16. Joe Lee Davis, "Richard Brome's Neglected Contribution to Comic Theory," *Studies in Philology* XXX (1943), 520-28. Professor Davis expands his comparison of *The Antipodes* and *The Muse's Looking Glass* in "Thalia's Double Image," Chapter two in *The Sons of Ben* (Detroit, 1967), pp. 59-80.

17. For an account of the importance of *The Floating Island* in contemporary religious and political controversy, consult Bentley, V, 1189-95.

18. Ian Donaldson, *The World Upside-Down* (Oxford, 1970), p. 81.

19. The whole of the paragraph from which Donaldson quotes is as follows:

But should one wish to examine more elaborately the question of the Antipodes, he would easily find them to be old wives' fables. For if two men on opposite sides placed the soles of their feet each against each, whether they chose to stand on earth, or water, or air, or fire, or any other kind of body, how could both be found standing upright? The one would be assuredly found in the natural upright position, and the other, contrary to nature, head downward. Such positions are opposed to reason, and alien to our nature and condition. And how, again, when it rains upon both of them, is it possible to say that the rain falls down upon the two, and not that it falls down to the one and up to the other, or falls against them, or towards them, or away from them. For to think that there are Antipodes compels us to think also that rain falls on them from an opposite direction to ours; and any one will, with good reason, deride these ludicrous theories, which set forth principles incongruous, ill-adjusted, and contrary to nature. (John Watson McCrindle, ed., *The Christian Topography of Cosmas, Hakluyt Society*, O.S. XCVIII [London, 1897], 17)

We cannot expect, of course, that Brome or any other of his Renaissance contemporaries would necessarily know Cosmas, but, as McCrindle points out, "Nearly all the Christian fathers held the same opinion as Cosmas about the Antipodes" (loc. cit.), and through them the concept became a Renaissance commonplace.

20. Professor Donaldson devotes a chapter to discussing the relationship of Brome's *The Antipodes* to this theory of comedy (op. cit., pp. 82-98).

21. Or again,

Fac. And Lovers are as phantastic as ours?
2 Her. But none that will hang themselves for Love, or
eat candle ends, or drink to their Mistress' eyes, till
their own bid them good night, as the *Sublunary Lovers* do.
(Jonson, VII, 519-20)

22. Donaldson, op. cit., p. 78.

23. Swinburne, p. 335.

24. Bentley, III, 71-72.

25. William Van Lennep et al., eds., *The London Stage 1660-18* (Carbondale, Ill., 1960-68), I, i (1965), 31-46; and J. Q. Adams, op. cit., p. 118.

26. For the dates of these seventeenth- and eighteenth-century revivals both as a play and as a comic opera, consult *The London Stage*, passim.

27. Robert Clifford Latham and William Mathews, eds., *The Diary of*

Samuel Pepys (Berkeley and Los Angeles, 1970), II, 141.

28. J. A. Symonds, "Review of the Dramatic Works of Richard Brome," *Academy* V (March 21, 1874), 305 (école buissonière—hedgeschool; faire l'école buissonière—to play truant).

29. Thomas Marc Parrott and Robert Hamilton, *A Short View of English Drama* (New York, 1943), p. 178. For further comment on the green world quality of *A Jovial Crew*, consult Swinburne, p. 337, and Schelling, op. cit., p. 170.

30. Kaufmann, op. cit., p. 170.

31. OED, *doxy*. Originally the term in Vagabond's Cant for the unmarried mistress of a beggar or a rogue; a beggar's trull or wench.

32. OED, *Dell. Rogues' Cant. arch.* A young girl (of the vagrant class); a wench.

33. OED 5, *Mell.* To copulate. The OED cites this line as an example.

34. Professor Haaker explains in her edition of *A Jovial Crew* (Lincoln, Nebraska, 1968) that "whereas rents of farm lands increased threefold between 1600 and 1688, Oldrents generously allowed his tenants to continue at the old rate" (p. 15n). References are made throughout the play to his open-heartedness and kindness.

35. Jonson, VIII, 580–81.

Chapter Eight

1. Symonds, op. cit., p. 304. Professor Symonds exempted only *A Jovial Crew* from this judgment.

2. Allen's subtitle for *A Study of the Comedies of Richard Brome.*

3. Andrews, op. cit., p. 111.

4. Symonds, op. cit., p. 304.

5. Charles M. Gayley, *Representative English Comedies,* 3 vols. (New York, 1903–14), III, xci.

6. Kathleen Lynch, *The Social Mode of Restoration Comedy* (New York, 1926), p. 43.

7. Ibid., p. 188.

8. Thorndike, op. cit., p. 251.

9. Kaufmann, op. cit., p. 1.

10. Sedge, op. cit., p. 317.

11. Clifford Leech, "The Caroline Audience," Chapter 8 in *Shakespeare's Tragedies and Other Studies in Seventeenth Century Drama* (London, 1950), p. 160.

12. Eric Bentley, *The Life of the Drama* (New York, 1967), pp. 40–41.

13. Parrot and Ball, op. cit., p. 175.

14. Jonson, III, 432.

15. Sedge, op. cit., p. 130.

16. Prologue to *The Novella* (sig. H 4^v).

Selected Bibliography

PRIMARY SOURCES

1. Individual Works

The Antipodes: a Comedy. Printed by *J. Okes,* for *Francis Constable,* and are to be sold at his shops in Kings-street at the sign of the Goat, and in Westminster-hall (London, 1640).

Five New Plays, viz. The *Mad Couple Well Matcht. Novella. Court Begger. City Wit. Damoiselle.* Printed for *Humphrey Moseley, Richard Marriot,* and *Thomas Dring,* and are to be sold at their Shops (London, 1653).

Five New Plays, viz. *The English Moor, or The Mock-Marriage. The Love-sick Court, or The Ambitious Politique. Covent Garden Weeded. The New Academy, or The New Exchange. The Queen and Concubine.* Printed for *A. Crook* at the Green Dragon in Saint *Paul's* Church-yard, and for *H. Brome* at the Gunn in Ivy-lane (London, 1659).

A Jovial Crew: or, The Merry Beggars. Printed by *J.Y.* for *E.D.* and *N.E.* and are to be sold at the Gun in *Ivy-Lane* (London, 1652).

The Northern Lass, a Comedy. Printed by Aug. Mathews, and are to be sold by Nicholas Vavasor, dwelling at the little South door of St. *Paul's* Church (London, 1632).

The Queen's Exchange, a Comedy. Printed for *Henry Brome* at the Hand in *Paul's Churchyard* (London, 1657).

The Sparagus Garden: a Comedy. Printed by *J. Okes,* for Francis Constable, and are to be sold at his shops in Kings-street at the sign of the Goat, and in Westminster-hall (London, 1640).

2. Collaboration

HEYWOOD, THOMAS, and BROME, RICHARD. *The Late Lancashire Witches.* Printed by *Thomas Harper* for *Benjamin Fisher,* and are to be sold at his Shop at the Sign of the *Talbot,* without *Aldersgate* (London, 1634).

3. Collection

Lachrymae Musarum; The Tears of the Muses. Collected and set forth by R. B. Printed by *Thomas Newcomb* (London, 1649).

163

SECONDARY SOURCES

ADAMS, JOSEPH QUINCY, ed. *The Dramatic Records of Sir Henry Herbert 1623-1673*. New Haven: Yale University Press, 1917. Sir Henry Herbert's office-book (no longer extant) covered the period 1622-42 during which he was Master of the Revels. Among other relevant documents, Adams brings together quotations from it which appear dispersed throughout the works of Edmund Malone and George Chalmers.

ALLEN, HERBERT F. *A Study of the Comedies of Richard Brome: Especially as Representative of Dramatic Decadence*. Stanford: Stanford University Press, 1912. Originally a University of Michigan thesis, the critical attitudes expressed are out of date and based upon a questionable definition of decadence.

ANDREWS, CLARENCE EDWARD. *Richard Brome: A Study of His Life and Works*. New York: Henry Holt and Company, 1913. Part of the *Yale Studies in English Series*, this work originally prefaced a dissertation edition of *The Antipodes*. The author's interest in his subject is historic rather than intrinsic.

BENTLEY, GERALD EADES. *The Jacobean and Caroline Stage*. 7 vols. London: Oxford University Press, 1941-68. This monumental work follows on from E. K. Chambers's *Elizabethan Drama* and is indispensable to anyone working in Renaissance Drama.

CLARK, ARTHUR MELVILLE. *Thomas Heywood: Playwright and Miscellanist*. Oxford: Basil Blackwell, 1931. A solid scholarly study of Heywood in which the critic credits Brome for what dramatic merit *The Late Lancashire Witches* has.

COPE, JACKSON I. "Richard Brome: The World as Antipodes," in *The Theater and the Dream: From Metaphor to Form in Renaissance Drama*. Baltimore and London: The Johns Hopkins University Press, 1973. A highly complex theoretical study of the manner in which the metaphors "all the world's a stage" and life "is such stuff as dreams are made on" relate to dramatic structure and to art as a reflection of human experience. Includes discussion of *The Queen's Exchange, The English Moor, The Antipodes*, and *A Jovial Crew*. Shorter comments on *The Queen and Concubine* and *The Novella* appear in the notes. "Brome is the most accomplished and serious dramatist between the Jacobean masters and Dryden."

DAVIS, JOE LEE. "Richard Brome's Neglected Contribution to Comic Theory," *Studies in Philology* XXXX (1943), 520-28. Excellent study of *The Antipodes*'s comic theory as "cathartic" and "extra-realistic," inspired by Thomas Randolph's *The Muses' Looking Glass* (1630).

——. *The Sons of Ben*. Detroit: Wayne State University Press, 1967. This work includes comment on eleven of Brome's plays as well as

selected works by Henry Glapthorne, Peter Hausted, Thomas
Killigrew, Shackerley Marmion, Jasper Mayne, Thomas Nabbes,
and Thomas Randolph. Professor Davis sees only Brome's *The
Antipodes* and Randolph's *The Muses' Looking Glass* as standing
apart from the plays of these "minor dramatists" or "small fry."

DONALDSON, IAN. " 'Living Backward': *The Antipodes,*" in *The World
Upside-Down: Comedy from Jonson to Fielding.* Oxford: Clarendon Press, 1970. Critical study of *The Antipodes* relating it to
traditional views of the antipodes as a locale of physical and moral
opposites and to the theory of comic inversion.

FLETCHER, JEFFERSON BUTLER. "Precieuses at the Court of Charles I,"
Journal of Comparative Literature I (1903), 120–53. Includes
Brome among satiric opponents of the Neo-Platonic love cult in the
court of Charles I.

GREG, W. W. *A Bibliography of the English Printed Drama to the
Restoration.* 4 vols. London: Oxford University Press, 1939–59.
The title of this work is self-explanatory and its reputation as an
indispensable bibliographic tool is firmly established.

HAAKER, ANN. "The Plague, the Theatre, and the Poet," *Renaissance
Drama* n.s. I (1968), 283–306. Documentary and historical
discussion of the legal disputes between Brome and the Salisbury
Court Theatre in 1640 which reveals much basic information on
Caroline Playwrights' contracts with theaters.

INGRAM, R. W. "The Musical Art of Richard Brome's Comedies,"
Renaissance Drama n.s. VII (1976), 219–42. This study gives credit
to Brome for his skill in incorporating music and musical
entertainments as integral parts of total dramatic impression.

JONSON, BEN. *The New Inn or The Light Heart.* Edited with Introduction,
Notes, and Glossary by George Bremner Tennant. *Yale Studies in
English* XXXIV (1908). New York: Henry Holt and Company.

———. *Works.* Edited by C. H. Herford, Percy and Evelyn Simpson. 11
vols. Oxford: Clarendon Press, 1925–51.

KAUFMANN, R. J. *Richard Brome: Caroline Dramatist.* New York and
London: Columbia University Press, 1961. A good modern critical
study of some of Brome's works which, although claiming to
present a "sympathetic account of Brome's seventeenth century
conservatism," does credit Brome with some creative originality
and independent artistic consciousness.

LYNCH, KATHLEEN. *The Social Mode of Restoration Comedy.* New York:
The Macmillan Company, 1926. Traces gradual shifts in moral
attitudes and comic standards from the late Elizabethan period
through the Restoration and concludes that the drama of Ethridge,
Congreve, and their contemporaries is part of a developmental
process of which Brome is a part.

MILES, THEODORE. "Place-Realism in a Group of Caroline Plays," *Review of English Studies* XVIII (1942), 428-40. Includes Brome's *Covent-Graden Weeded* and *Sparagus Garden* among contemporary vogue of realistic plays dealing with specific London areas.

NICOLL, ALLARDYCE, and BOSWELL, ELEANORE, eds. "Dramatic Records: The Lord Chamberlain's Office," *Malone Society Collections*, general editor W. W. Greg, II: 3 (1931), 321-416. Basic theatrical records from 1619 to 1637, including Brome as Queen of Bohemia's player and listing performances of *The Late Lancashire Witches* and *The Love-sick Maid*.

PERKINSON, RICHARD H. "Topographical Comedy in the Seventeenth Century," *English Literary History* III (1936), 270-90. Relates earlier topographical comedies to Restoration in the use of realistic settings as plausible backgrounds for comedies of manners.

SENSABAUGH, GEORGE. "Platonic Court Drama," *Huntington Library Quarterly* I (1937-38), 277-99. Background study of tenets, ethics, and criticism of Neo-Platonic love cult at Caroline court.

SWINBURNE, ALGERNON CHARLES. "Richard Brome," in *The Complete Works* XII (1926), 326-38. Sir Edmund Gosse and Thomas J. Wise, eds., 20 vols. London: William Heineman Ltd., 1925-27. Highly stylized Victorian evaluations of Brome's plays, comparing him unfavorably to Jonson.

SYMONDS, JOHN ADDINGTON. "Review of the Dramatic Works of Richard Brome," *Academy* V (March 21, 1874), 304-305. Extremely negative view of Brome as a "lackey" to Ben Jonson.

THALER, ALWIN. "Was Richard Brome an Actor?" *Modern Language Notes* XXXVI (1921), 88-91. Argues Brome as actor from his inclusion in 1628 in a royal warrant to the Queen of Bohemia's players.

WEDGWOOD, C. V. "Comedy in the Reign of Charles I," *Studies in Social History*. J. H. Plumb, ed. London: Longmans, Green and Company, 1955, pp. 109-37. Relates specific motifs of Caroline comedy to topics of contemporary society.

Index